# Pathways
# TOWARDS
## NON AGGRESSION

New You

Old You

New Beginning

Dr. Thomas (Thom) Glaza
Melanie (Mel) Mason

PAGE PUBLISHING, INC.
New York, NY

First originally published by Page Publishing, Inc. 2018

ISBN 978-1-64082-372-3 (Paperback)
ISBN 978-1-64082-373-0 (Digital)

Printed in the United States of America

# THE ORIGINS

In our minds, fate brings people together no matter how apart they may be, whether it be geographical, age, or professional paths. We had no intention of setting out on the wondrous journey that we experienced in the summer of 2016. As the days and weeks passed, we were provided with an incredible opportunity—developing a tool that would help countless others experience personal growth and achieve contentment in their lives. This focus kept us inspired during our adventure.

In May 2016, I was searching for an organization where I could volunteer my services during the summer months before commencing my senior year at the University of Florida. I had been struggling to find the right career path for myself as applying for graduate school was right around the corner. Somewhat on a whim, I decided to apply for an internship position at Tri-County Counseling and Life Skills Center. I had always loved serving others, and I had hoped it would be a good opportunity to see firsthand the work that counselors perform on a daily basis. What I soon discovered is that my time at Tri-County Counseling would be so much more than that.

*Melanie "Mel" Mason*

In May 2016, Melanie "Mel" Mason contacted Tri-County Counseling and Life Skills Center Inc., in North Port, Florida, where I am the founder, CEO, and clinical director, seeking to volunteer. I met with Mel and was immediately impressed with her intelligence, affability, and overall demeanor. For several years, the dream of creating "the great American workbook" had been floating in and out of my consciousness. I shared this dream with Mel, who challenged and encouraged me to make it a reality. Without Mel's guidance and assistance, this workbook would never have been published.

*Dr. Thomas (Thom) Glaza*

Initially, we focused on developing a workbook for clients who presented with issues of anger, aggression, or violence. We soon discovered that this was not the best use of our combined skill sets. We focused on developing a self-improvement tool for the masses. We then reviewed a variety of products, hoping to identify a format that met our needs. A number of items were pleasing to the eye—lots of colorful graphics—but were lacking in substance. We ruled out formats that were directive in nature (e.g., "you must," "you have to"). Some just were not user-friendly, while others were cost-prohibitive.

We surmised that we needed to create a workbook presenting topics that affect all of us, in a language that was inclusive rather than exclusive. The workbook would be easily understood, with graphics that did not detract from substance, and with a cost that was truly affordable.

We invested approximately three hundred hours of research, labor, and many rewrites and finished with a product we are immensely proud. We were fortunate to meet Jason Dorsey, who kindly donated his skills in graphic design. With Jason's artistic mastery, we had a tangible product we felt would inspire and energize a cross section of society.

It is our hope that your journey through this workbook is an enjoyable one and that it provides you with a higher degree of self-enlightenment.

# Contents

## Section 9   Conflict Resolution

## Section 10 A New Beginning

NOTE: All "Fun Fact" graphics located throughout the workbook have been found from multiple sources, including but not limited to Noel Botham's *The Mega Book of Useless Information* and Did You Know?'s Fast Facts.

# Preparation Work—Timeline of Major Life Events

Before starting on your path toward self-enlightenment, it is important for you to understand the decisive circumstances and occurrences in your lives that led you to where you are today. It is imperative that you complete this preparation work before you begin Section 1 of the *Pathways toward Non-Aggression* workbook. We believe that you will find yourself referring back to this exercise when completing Section assignments.

When we write down our life's experiences, we can no longer deny that our environment (family of origin, socioeconomics, physical health, educational level, belief system, mental and emotional health, etc.) had a major impact on molding the person we have become. Creating your own timeline will provide you with insight as to how life events have contributed to your past and current attitudes, behaviors, and decision-making. Essentially, how these events helped or hindered you from developing your unique personality will become critical when assessing your needs and areas to improve throughout this workbook.

We encourage you to be thorough with this exercise. When you believe that you have captured all the relevant situations, we recommend that you solicit the assistance of significant others (e.g., parents/guardians, siblings, spouses/mates, mentors, etc.) to help you recall important life experiences that you may have forgotten or that you might have suppressed. (Sometimes we relegate to the farthest reaches of our minds those events that caused us pain; people, places and events that we would rather forget).

*If you find yourself dredging up suppressed memories that cause you to feel an unacceptable degree of discomfort, please seek the assistance of a licensed mental health counselor before going any further with this exercise.

We have provided you with a sample timeline (next page), to help you get started on your journey of discovery.

# Timeline of Major Life Events

## *Examples*

Birth_____3_____5_____9_____12_____17_____21_____Present

Age 3. My dad went back to work (he was a stay-at-home parent). I was put in a preschool program across town and had to take a bus. I'd never ridden a bus or been to that part of town. I didn't know any of the kids in my class. None of them were from my neighborhood. I was scared, hurt, and lonely. I cried every day.
(Negative experiences)

Age 5. My mother was promoted by her company. We had to move to another town, but it wasn't far away so I could still spend time with my grandparents, uncles and aunts, and cousins. Because Mom was making more money, we bought our first house. In the apartment, I had to share my room, but in the house, I had my own room. We also bought our first dog.
(Positive experiences)

Age 9. My parents separated. I was confused and hurt. They tried to reassure me that it had nothing to do with me, but I still blamed myself. I lived with Dad during the week and Mom on the weekends. They lived far apart, so I couldn't play with my friends on the weekends. They divorced, and Mom moved to another state. I knew a lot of kids were going through the same thing, but they seemed to be okay with it. I felt like my mom abandoned me. I tried to talk to my parents about my feelings. They didn't seem to care.
(Negative experiences)

Age 12. My dad had a new girlfriend. Before they decided to get married, he and his girlfriend sat us down and talked to us about how this would affect our lives. I liked the idea because now I would have a live-in mother. My dad was happier than he had been in a long time. We helped plan their wedding reception.
(Positive experiences)

Age 17. My stepmother became pregnant. She and my dad were really happy. They were always talking about the "new baby." To be honest, I was jealous. It seemed like all

their attention went to the baby. I felt invisible. They made me babysit. I quit school and moved in with a friend's family.
(Negative experiences)

Age 17. I went to a party at a friend's house, when her parents were out of town. She had plenty of alcohol and drugs. I smoked pot for the very first time. It made me forget my problems. It really relaxed me.
(Negative or positive experiences?)

Age 21. I became engaged to a wonderful person who encouraged me to obtain a GED, change my nowhere job, and go back to school. I've never had anyone who I could open up to and who cared about my happiness.
(Positive experiences)

# Timeline of Major Life Events

Write in the most important events (positive and negative) in your
life, at the ages they occurred, on the timeline below.

Birth _____ Present

Place each of the events you listed above in the categories:
positive experiences and negative experiences.

| POSITIVE EXPERIENCES | NEGATIVE EXPERIENCES |
|---|---|
| | |
| | |
| | |
| | |
| | |
| | |
| | |

# Section 1:
# Building Character

# BUILDING CHARACTER

In order to truly grow as individuals, we must understand the personal values (also known as character) that drive our attitudes, which in turn drive our behaviors. *Character counts* posits that there are six pillars upon which personal character is built. They are respect, trustworthiness, fairness, caring, responsibility, and citizenship. For the purpose of this section, we have expanded this concept, providing you with thirty-seven character traits, along with their opposing traits (e.g., benevolence vs. selfishness, sincerity vs. dishonesty, truthfulness vs. deception). It is our hope that you will identify your character strengths and weaknesses and develop a plan to enhance your strengths and minimize your weaknesses, with the intent of improving your quality of life and the quality of life of those around you.

# Objectives

At the end of this section, the participant will be able to

1.  verbalize a clear understanding of your values/character traits and how they contribute to your attitudes and behaviors,
2.  verbalize a clear understanding of how your character traits affect your attitudes and behaviors,
3.  identify the healthy traits that strengthen your character, and
4.  identify the unhealthy traits that weaken your character.

# PERSONAL CHARACTERISTICS

Character is defined as "the mental and moral qualities distinctive to an individual." A value is defined as "the regard that something is held to deserve; the importance, worth, or usefulness of something" or "a person's principles or standards of behavior; one's judgment of what is important in life."

For the purpose of this exercise, we have combined the definitions into what we term Personal Characteristics. To assist you, we have defined each characteristic, and provided you with the opposite trait.

Why do we have a separate section on personal characteristics/values? Simply because our values form our attitudes, which are manifested in our behaviors.

As to personal values, we believe that there are three types: complete, partial, and false. A complete value is defined as a high standard of behavior that we hold ourselves to (e.g., I will not cheat, steal, violate a law, etc.). You have been given opportunities where you could violate this standard and not get caught yet repeatedly remained committed to this value.

A partial value is defined as a standard of behavior that we hold ourselves to, yet our resolve has yet to be tested. In other words, we aren't 100% certain that we would remain faithful to the standard, if we were given the opportunity to violate it and not get caught.

A false value can be defined in two ways: (1) holding others who we have power over to a standard of behavior that we do not apply to ourselves or (2) rationalizing minor violations of our own standards because they weren't major infractions. As to the first definition, one example would be telling your children that they should never smoke cigarettes, punishing them when caught, yet you continue to smoke. Or teaching your children that you will punish them if they lie, yet you lied to your boss about being sick and need the day off, when what you are really doing is taking the day to go fishing. Another example is employers or managers who demand certain behaviors of their employees, yet they themselves regularly violate these standards (e.g., be at work on time, give a full day's work, be respectful, etc.).

As to the second definition, what about stealing? Some people would never steal from a family member, a friend, or a coworker, yet they have stolen something (regardless of the monetary value) from a "big box store" because "it doesn't really hurt them." Then there are those people who rationalize an unacceptable behavior because "everyone does it." What about the person who smokes marijuana yet justifies the behavior because "it isn't as bad as cocaine or heroin."

 **FUN FACT** Emerging research about brain development suggests that most people do not reach full maturity in their brain until the age of 25.

Before you begin the personal characteristics self-assessment, let's take a look at some examples of the connectivity of values, attitudes, and behaviors.

## Example 1

| | |
|---|---|
| Positive behavior | A smoker placing his cigarette butts in the proper receptacles |
| Suggested attitude | "I need to clean up after myself." |
| Possible values | Orderliness, responsibility, self-control |
| Negative behavior | A smoker disposing his cigarette butts wherever he chooses |
| Suggested attitude | "Other people get paid to clean up after me." |
| Consequences | Confusion, unreliability, self-indulgence |

## Example 2

| | |
|---|---|
| Positive behavior | Being on time for work and appointments |
| Suggested attitude | "I want to be seen as being responsible." (Effective time management) |
| Possible values | Dependability, orderliness, punctuality, responsibility |
| Negative behavior | Frequently being late for appointments or work |
| Suggested attitude | "I can't seem to get my act together." |
| Consequences | Inconsistency, confusion, tardiness, unreliability |

## Example 3

| | |
|---|---|
| Positive behavior | Volunteering time and skills to help a nonprofit organization |
| Suggested attitude | "I want/need to give to others less fortunate than myself." |
| Possible values | Availability, compassion, sympathy, generosity |
| Negative behavior | Not helping or reaching out to others |
| Suggested attitude | "I'm not going to give anyone my time and skills for free." |
| Consequences | Self-centeredness, indifference, stinginess |

## Example 4

| | |
|---|---|
| Positive behavior | Eating healthy, exercising three times a week, and keeping my mind active |
| Suggested attitude | "I must care for myself so that I can nurture a healthy body and mind." |
| Possible values | Healthiness, concern, responsibility, attentiveness |
| Negative behavior | Eating junk food, not regularly exercising, and using narcotic substances frequently |
| Suggested attitude | "I don't have time to take care of myself. I'm too busy working." |
| Consequences | Substance abuse, obesity, sickness, wasted potential |

Step 1. Place a "C" next to your complete character traits.

Step 2. Place a "P" next to your partial character traits.

Step 3. Place an "F" next to your false character traits.

Step 4. In the tables given below, describe how long you have held each of these traits and in recent months with whom and where you have practiced this trait. Describe with whom and where you will strengthen this positive character trait.

Examples:

Tolerance. "I will readily admit to myself when I am intolerant of someone who has different beliefs than mine and work on being more accepting."

Attentiveness. "I will be quiet, listen, and not interrupt when others are speaking." "I will ask questions if I don't understand what the person is saying."

Shifting from Anger to Security. "I will not project what might or might not happen in the future, and do what I can today to feel secure."

# CHARACTERISTICS AND THEIR OPPOSITES

_____ Attentiveness. Possessing and utilizing effective listening skills; giving others my undivided attention; asking clarifying questions when I don't understand what the other person is telling me.
   Opposite of Attentiveness: Distraction

_____ Availability. Being approachable and available to people who need or want my attention, my guidance, my advice, or my assistance.
   Opposite of Availability: Self-Centeredness

_____ Benevolence. The act of attending to the needs of others, without any ulterior motive; doing something for someone else without repayment of any kind.
   Opposite of Benevolence: Selfishness

_____ Boldness. Having confidence in knowing that my thoughts and actions are true, right, and just.

    Opposite of Boldness: Fearfulness

_____ Caution. Considering the implications of important decisions before taking any action.

    Opposite of Caution: Impulsiveness

_____ Compassion. Doing whatever I need to do in order to help heal the pain that others are feeling; to not intentionally cause anyone else emotional pain.

    Opposite of Compassion: Indifference

_____ Contentment. Realizing and living my life with the belief that true happiness does not depend on my collecting material things.

    Opposite of Contentment: Dissatisfaction

_____ Creativity. Seeking out new and innovative ways to improve my spiritual, emotional, mental, and physical well-being.

    Opposite of Creativity: Underachievement

_____ Decisiveness. The ability to make difficult decisions in a timely and efficient manner.

    Opposite of Decisiveness: Procrastination

_____ Deference. Respecting the views and preferences of others when they differ from or are in conflict with my own views and preferences.

    Opposite of Deference: Impoliteness

_____ Dependability. Fulfilling what I committed myself to accomplish, even when it may result in an unexpected sacrifice.

    Opposite of Dependability: Inconsistency

_____ Determination. Establishing clear-cut, realistic, achievable goals and accomplishing them, even when others attempt to interfere with or sabotage my plans.

    Opposite of Determination: Faintheartedness

_____ Discretion. Recognizing and avoiding words and actions that could bring undesirable consequences to me or to others.

    Opposite of Discretion: Carelessness

_____ Endurance. The inner strength to withstand stress and to do my best.

    Opposite of Endurance: Idleness

_____ Faith. The confidence that my actions are right and true and that they will yield the best outcome, even though I cannot foresee what the outcome might be.

    Opposite of Faith: Distrust

_____ Flexibility. The ability to adapt or to change my plans and ideas as the situations and people around me change.

    Opposite of Flexibility: Resistance

_____ Forgiveness. Refraining from holding a grudge for a real or perceived slight; not letting another person's behavior make me feel bad about myself.

    Opposite of Forgiveness: Resentment

_____ Generosity. Sharing my knowledge and assets with others so that they may achieve a higher level of emotional, mental, and spiritual well-being.

    Opposite of Generosity: Selfishness

_____ Gratefulness. Letting others know, by my words and deeds, that I truly appreciate the ways that they have helped me to live a more fulfilling life.

    Opposite of Gratefulness: Criticism

_____ Honor. Showing respect and appreciation for other people, regardless of their station in life.

    Opposite of Honor: Disrespect

_____ Humility. Overtly recognize and give credit to those individuals who have helped me with the successes that I have achieved thus far in life.

    Opposite of Humility: Arrogance

_____ Initiative. Possessing the self-motivation to accomplish a task, find new solutions to an old problem, and seek new ways to better myself.

Opposite of Initiative: Idleness

_____ Joyfulness. Maintaining a positive attitude toward life, even when faced with unpleasant conditions.

Opposite of Joyfulness: Unhappiness

_____ Justice. To behave in a manner that is pure, right, and true while encouraging others to do the same.

Opposite of Justice: Corruption

_____ Loyalty. Showing my commitment to those ideals and individuals whom I support, especially during difficult times.

Opposite of Loyalty: Unfaithfulness

_____ Patience. Accepting a difficult or pressing situation and showing a willingness to wait for events to fall into place, in their own time.

Opposite of Patience: Impatience

_____ Punctuality. Showing esteem for myself and others by being on time for work, appointments, meetings, etc.

Opposite of Punctuality: Tardiness

_____ Responsibility. Knowing what is expected of me and carrying out those duties without being asked.

Opposite of Responsibility: Unreliability

_____ Security. Structuring my life in such a way that I feel emotionally, mentally, physically, and spiritually safe.

Opposite of Security: Uncertainty

_____ Self-Control. Refraining from acting on impulsive thoughts, without considering their long-term impact on my life.

Opposite of Self-Control: Self-Indulgence

_____ Sensitivity. Perceiving correctly the attitudes and emotions of others.
Opposite of Sensitivity: Apathy

_____ Serenity. Remaining calm and productive, especially when faced with difficult or unexpected situations.
Opposite of Serenity: Disturbance

_____ Sincerity. To do what is right, without any hidden motives.
Opposite of Sincerity: Dishonesty

_____ Thriftiness. Spending money on what is necessary to enhance my emotional, mental, physical, and spiritual well-being.
Opposite of Thriftiness: Extravagance

_____ Tolerance. Realizing that every human being is at a different level of character development; accepting where others are at without trying to change them.
Opposite of Tolerance: Intolerance

_____ Truthfulness. Being honest with myself and with others, even when there may be negative consequences for my actions.
Opposite of Truthfulness: Deception

_____ Wisdom. Understanding and responding to life's situations, and taking actions that will hold up to close scrutiny.
Opposite of Wisdom: Foolishness

 Most of the privileges and responsibilities of adulthood are legally granted by the age of 18. However, critical parts of the brain involved in decision-making are not fully developed until years later at the age of 25 or so.

## Please continue onto the next two pages for the Personal Characteristics Assessment tool.

| Those Traits Labeled "C" | Those Traits Labeled "P" | Those Traits Labeled "F" |
|---|---|---|
| Complete (Strong) Positive Character Traits | Partially (Weak) Positive Character Traits | False (Unhealthy) Character Traits |
| | | |
| | | |
| | | |
| | | |
| | | |
| | | |
| | | |
| | | |
| | | |
| | | |
| | | |
| | | |
| | | |

# Traits Labeled "C"

Complete Positive Character Traits

Out of the complete positive character traits that you identified, choose the top three traits you feel are your strongest.

*Please elaborate on these traits.

Trait 1: _____

Why I possess this trait: _____

_____

I have held this trait since: _____

I will strengthen this trait by: _____

Trait 2: _____

Why I possess this trait: _____

_____

I have held this trait since: _____

I will strengthen this trait by: _____

Trait 3: _____

Why I possess this trait: _____

_____

I have held this trait since: _____

I will strengthen this trait by: _____

## Traits Labeled "P"

Partially Positive Character Traits

Out of the partially, positive character traits listed above, please choose the three traits you feel are your strongest.

*Please elaborate on these traits.

Trait 1: _____

Why I possess this trait: _____

_____

I have held this trait since: _____

I will strengthen this trait by: _____

Trait 2: _____

Why I possess this trait: _____

_____

I have held this trait since: _____

I will strengthen this trait by: _____

Trait 3: _____

Why I possess this trait: _____

_____

I have held this trait since: _____

I will strengthen this trait by: _____

"The greatest day in your life and mine is when we take total responsibility for our attitudes. That's the day we truly grow up." – John C. Maxwell

# Traits Labeled "F"

False Character Traits

Out of the false character traits listed above, please choose the three traits you feel that you need to change.

*Please elaborate on these traits.

Trait 1: _____

Why I possess this trait: _____

_____

I have held this train since: _____

I will strengthen this trait by: _____

Trait 2: _____

Why I possess this trait: _____

_____

I have held this trait since: _____

I will strengthen this trait by: _____

Trait 3: _____

Why I possess this trait: _____

_____

I have held this trait since: _____

I will strengthen this trait by: _____

# Section 2:
# Gender and Society

# GENDER AND SOCIETY

It is safe to say that all human beings are the product of gender role socialization, whether consciously or subconsciously. Gender roles are based on the different expectations that individuals, groups, and societies have of individuals based on their sex. Gender socialization, then, is preparing an individual to fulfill her or his assigned roles. Yet in our advancing society, these traditional gender roles are starting to be questioned. Should men and women have the same opportunities, responsibilities, and chances at success?

## Objectives

At the end of this section, the participant will be able to
1.  identify gender biases in your life and environment,
2.  identify the sources of overt and covert gender biases,
3.  identify what impact gender bias had and continues to have on your lives,
4.  identify your own gender biases, and
5.  identify ways you can actively support gender equality.

# GENDER AND SOCIETY ⚥

It is safe to say that all human beings are the product of gender socialization, whether consciously or subconsciously. Gender roles are determined by the expectations that individuals, groups, and societies have of individuals based on their sex and society's beliefs about gender. Gender socialization, then, is preparing an individual to fulfill her or his ascribed roles.

The terms *gender* and *sex* are often confused with one another. They are different concepts. Sex is a biological concept, determined on the basis of individuals' primary sex characteristics. Gender, on the other hand, refers to the meanings, values, and characteristics that people ascribe to different sexes.

In American society, the clothing we wear, the toys we play with as children, the way we interact with others, our parenting style, and even our career path can be predetermined based solely on our gender if we are subjected to the socialization that teaches us women's roles versus men's roles.

The act of gender socialization begins when an infant (or an embryo) is identified as being either female or male. The parents-to-be prepare for the arrival of their child in a variety of ways. They select a gender-specific name, purchase gender-specific clothing that adheres to a predetermined color scheme, decorate the baby's room in a gender-specific fashion, purchase gender-specific toys, and fantasize about a gender-specific career.

———————————————— *First Names* ————————————————

• Selecting a name that identifies the infant as a male or female is an established practice that can be traced back to early civilization, with few exceptions. When we hear an individual's first name, we subconsciously attach a gender to that individual. And, we are confused with first names that can apply to a female or a male. Is Billie a boy or a girl? How about Pat, Tony, Asia, Christian, Frankie, Jan, Bautista, Jada, Taylor, Ashley, Devon, Sam, Malik, Elijah, Jean, Andrés, or Erin?

# Clothing

- Why are girls dressed in pink and boys dressed in blue? Actually, this is a rather modern practice. For most of history, baby boys and girls wore the same, very practical, white articles of clothing. Clothing had to be functional and durable, passed down from one child to the next, regardless of gender. It wasn't until the nineteenth century that clothing in color began to appear. And, at least initially, colors were not gender-specific.

- A June 1918 *Ladies' Home Journal* article made the pronouncement that the color pink is for boys and blue is for girls, promoting the idea that pink is a "stronger" color, thus more suitable for boys. Blue, being a more delicate and dainty color, was thought to be "prettier" on girls. However, not everyone subscribed to this philosophy. Some believed that a child's hair color and clothing should match. Blue was thought to be a flattering color for a blond-haired child, while pink was flattering to brunettes. Others thought that a child's eye color and clothing should match—blue for blue-eyed children and pink for brown-eyed children. Would green then be the appropriate color for a child with hazel eyes?

- In 1927, a *Time Magazine* article contained a chart identifying gender-specific colors for boys and girls, advising parents to dress their sons in pink, a concept already being promoted by the leading clothiers of the day (Marshall Field in Chicago, Best & Co. in New York, Filene's in Boston, and Halle's in Cleveland).

- In the mid-1940s, American clothing manufacturers found that affluent parents were buying a whole new set of baby products when a second or third child was born—an opportune time to manufacture clothing of various colors. It is believed that the birth of the girls-wear-pink and boys-wear-blue practice evolved from clothing company catalogs repeatedly depicting girls dressed entirely in pink, and boys in blue. The fad rapidly spread, with people at all socioeconomic levels following this new trend. The gender-specific clothing tradition, even in the absence of scientific reasoning, continues to this day, and there have been very few attempts to challenge the status quo.

- An alternative mode of dress—unisex clothing—came into style in the USA during the 1960s and 1970s, about the same time as the women's liberation movement was taking foothold. While the concept of dressing children in gender-neutral clothing was somewhat appealing, especially from a financial point of view, the movement was relatively short-lived.

In the 1980s, prenatal testing emerged, permitting women to identify the gender of their child in utero. Baby nurseries could now be adorned in "appropriate" colors, and gender-appropriate clothing could be purchased well in advance of the baby's arrival. In modernity, birthing centers, hospital maternity wards, clothing stores, aunts and uncles, siblings, grandparents, and friends continue to perpetuate this tradition.

## Toys

- Gender socialization is not restricted to the color of clothing that we wear. Consider the selection of toys. Until quite recently, toys were marketed specifically for girls or for boys, and few if any were considered gender-inclusive. One train of thought is that children are naturally inclined toward gender-specific products. Another is that preferences for gender-specific toys is somehow genetically engineered. Since this preference is not observed in infants, gender socialization appears to explain preferences better than genetic predisposition.

- Research conducted by the National Association for the Education of Young Children discovered that toys made specifically for boys are associated with violence, danger, and competition, while toys for girls are meant to teach nurturing behaviors, physical attractiveness, and domestic skills. Since males throughout history have been expected to be aggressive and competitive throughout their lives, one can understand why male-oriented toys serve to help in the development of these skills. Given that females have been traditionally prepared to fulfill nurturing roles (e.g., stay-at-home mother, nursing, teaching, office work, etc.), one can readily understand why dolls, cookware, and domestic skills were necessary in order to prepare them for their role in society.

- It can be troubling for a child who violates the gender-specific barrier. Girls who express a preference for action figures, guns, trucks, athletic equipment, etc., are deterred from this activity, and may be labeled "tomboys." Boys who are curious about dolls, cookware, or other "girly" pursuits are labeled "sissies," and their sexual orientation is brought into question.

- Studies have repeatedly shown that, when left alone, babies will play with any toy placed before them. Toddlers' selection of toys is influenced by their parents' and other adults' encouragements—a further step in the gender socialization process. Once socialized, as to which toys are appropriate and inappropriate for them to play with, boys and girls learn to reject those toys more closely associated with their opposite gender. This transition to gender-specific toys appears to occur much more rapidly among boys than it does among girls. As boys begin to meet with other boys their own age and increase their social support system, they learn that, to be accepted, they are required to engage in gender- and age-appropriate activities for fear of being rejected.

• Marketing strategies for genderless toys have been widely spread, but they have yet to catch on. Some department stores display toys in such a way that the child can view her or his options and choose whichever toy is most appealing to him or her.

## Titles

• Consider how society identifies our social status. There are a number of formal and informal titles that we use in our daily communication. While an adult female is traditionally assigned any number of monikers (e.g., Miss, Ms., or Mrs.), adult males, whether single or married, are addressed as Mister. When a woman introduces herself to another individual for the first time, her marital status is immediately revealed. For a man, the title of "Mr." gives him privacy over his marital status. These differences between titles are ingrained in our societal rules, giving men more freedom in social interactions than women.

• Next, let's address the issue of professional titles. In our society, we tend to use the appropriately ascribed titles when identifying males, followed by their surname (e.g., Dr. Menendez, Professor Mason, Pastor Sirhan, Rabbi Gomez, Judge Schultz, Officer Somalski, etc.). When addressing a female in the same profession, we often take the liberty of using her first name (e.g., Doctor Amelia, Professor Cecilia, Pastor Shakira, Rabbi Melissa, Judge Suzanne, Officer Priscilla, etc.), followed by their surname. When a female with a professional license or advanced degree marries, she has three choices: retain her maiden name, adopt her husband's surname, or use a hyphenated surname (e.g., Professor Hart-Stevenson). Dr. Jesus Francisco remains Dr. Jesus Francisco. Further, women with professional licenses or advanced degrees who later marry are often required to pay a fee to obtain a new license in her married or hyphenated name.

• To observe the aforementioned trend firsthand, tune in to National Geographic Wild's *The Incredible Dr. Pol*. Dr. Jan Pol, a male, is a veterinarian with a large practice situated in rural Michigan. Throughout the show, he is addressed by his formal title "Dr.

Pol," while the two female veterinarians are addressed with less-formal titles "Doctor Emily" and "Doctor Brenda" by Dr. Pol, veterinary technicians, other staff members, and animal owners of all ages. It is interesting to note that the two female veterinarians introduce themselves to new animal owners using these informal titles.

• Finally, there is the issue of society distinguishing males and females with titles that clearly identify them as being either female or male, with the identifiers different for children than for adults. Children under the age of eighteen are appropriately referred to as boys and girls, while those aged eighteen and older referred to as men and women. Then again, is that really the case? In many segments of our society, we often hear adult women of all ages referred to as girls. It probably would sound somewhat bizarre and would be perceived as offensive by most men, if they were repeatedly referred to as boys.

## Societal Roles

• Until the 1950s, adult females in the USA were expected to dress and behave in a manner that would attract suitors. They would select a potential mate, marry, and assume the role of homemaker. This role consisted of producing children, maintaining the home in a neat and orderly fashion, doing laundry, shopping for groceries and clothing, preparing meals, and assisting the children with their homework.

• At the same time, adult males were also in search of a potential mate. They would select a mate, marry, and assume the role of breadwinner. They worked outside of the home (requiring them to be absent from the home and family for long periods), maintained the family's finances, made all the family's major decisions, served as disciplinarian, and maintained the grounds exterior to the home.

• Following the misguided belief that "women will just get pregnant," women were discouraged from pursing a college degree or a career outside of the home. At the time, there were very few career opportunities for women, usually restricted to nursing, teaching, and secretarial fields.

• Women were prohibited from choosing career fields that required physical strength, stamina, cognitive skills, and leadership qualities. The women's movement of the 1960s and 1970s called into question unrealistic screening requirements that were developed with the intent of excluding females. Marital status was also a disqualifier. The prevailing myth was that woman could not possibly fulfill her role as mother if she was permitted to pursue a career. This same philosophy was not applied to married men and fathers.

- Membership in service organizations (e.g., Rotary International, Kiwanis, Lions Club, Elks, Toastmasters, Moose, etc.) have traditionally been fraternal in nature, as have most of our military organizations (Veterans of Foreign Wars, American Legion, etc.). Facing a rapid decline in membership, these organizations have extended memberships to women, in order to survive.

- During the 1980s and 1990s, society experienced a number of changes that blurred society's expectations of men and women. Among these changes were an increase in the number of single parents, separated or divorced couples sharing parenting responsibilities, more women entering the workforce on a full-time basis, an increasing number of women pursuing advanced degrees, fathers becoming stay-at-home dads, and women entering career fields that were traditionally all-male bastions. So many changes occurring at once contributed to a paradigm shift—causing us to redefine our roles.

- Single mothers and single fathers are now expected to balance a career with school, raising children, maintaining a household, shopping, helping with schoolwork, preparing meals, managing the family's finances, and mowing the lawn.

- It is not surprising to learn that gay and lesbian couples are much less likely to organize their lives in gendered ways, and research has found that lesbian couples are much more likely to share household duties on an equal basis.

- Research is just beginning to explore how gender interacts with other characteristics such as race, ethnicity, sexual orientation, and socioeconomics to affect diverse family experiences. For instance, women of color historically have had much stronger ties to the workforce because their incomes are needed for the family to achieve economic well-being. They have a long history of effectively balancing work and household responsibilities.

- Latino/Latina parents tend to socialize their daughters in ways that are marked by traditional gender-related expectations and messages. Research indicates that household activities, the freedom to pursue activities and gain access to privileges, and the pursuit of higher education continue to be ascribed based on an individual's gender. The societal roles of Latin men and women have not changed as dramatically as their European-American middle-class counterparts.

- Worldwide, many countries recognize that equal rights should exist between men and women. Many have produced regulations intended to fight discrimination and programs granting women access to health, education, and economic rights. However, the fact remains that women have fewer opportunities than men to benefit from economic development, with lower participation in the labor force.

- Even in the most advanced countries, women's wages average 73% of those of men. While the principle of gender equality in the workplace is generally accepted, discriminatory practices persist in many organizations despite regulations to fight it. Although research has found biological differences between the two sexes, it has found no sex to be more capable or skillful than the other. Women and men share cognitive skills and brain capacities. Thus, women and men should be treated equally in society. Gender bias is a major issue that we must work to eliminate in our society. Because gender biases are embedded in our culture, it is very difficult to eliminate them without involving men and women as two halves of the whole solution.

High heels were originally created for men and seen as "masculine" for a century. Persian soldiers wore high-heeled shoes in the name of necessity when riding horseback, since shooting an arrow from a saddle was easier with a heel to secure the foot in its strap. As the European elite became fascinated with the unfamiliar Persian culture, men adopted the horsemen's masculine footwear for their own (totally impractical) use around 1600.

# Self-Assessment

The purpose of this exercise is to determine if you possess traditional gender role beliefs. When you have circled your responses, and before tabulating your score, take a moment to reflect on how gender socialization has impacted you and others in your life.

1.  I do/do not support the practice of clothing girls in pink and boys in blue.
2.  I do/do not believe that a woman's role is in the home, not in the workplace.
3.  I do/do not believe that women can effectively serve in a combat role.
4.  I would/would not be comfortable in a role as stay-at-home dad.
5.  I do/do not believe that women are as effective as men in leadership roles.
6.  I do/do not believe that men should do laundry, even when living with a female.
7.  I do/do not believe that women should be allowed to play professional sports.
8.  I do/do not believe that women make better nurses than men.
9.  I do/do not believe that women are genetically predisposed to be more nurturing than men.
10. I do/do not support the concept of gender-specific toys.
11. I do/do not believe that the man should make major decisions for the family.
12. I do/do not believe that single mothers can effectively balance parenthood and a career.
13. I do/do not believe that single fathers can effectively balance parenthood and a career.
14. I do/do not believe that women can effectively balance parenthood and a career.
15. I do/do not believe that men work harder than women.
16. I do/do not believe that the value to society of men and women is equal.
17. I do/do not believe that women are the weaker sex.
18. I do/do not believe that wives should obey their husbands.
19. I do/do not believe that the man is the head of the household.
20. I do/do not believe that women belong in politics.

To obtain your score, transfer your do/do not selections from the previous page to the appropriate columns below. Give yourself one point for each item that you circled under the Gender-Neutral Response column. Add up your points to arrive at a final score.

| Item | Gender-Socialized Response | Gender-Neutral Response |
|------|----------------------------|-------------------------|
| 1. | do | do not |
| 2. | do | do not |
| 3. | do not | do |
| 4. | would not | would |
| 5. | do not | do |
| 6. | do not | do |
| 7. | do not | do |
| 8. | do | do not |
| 9. | do | do not |
| 10. | do | do not |
| 11. | do | do not |
| 12. | do not | do |
| 13. | do not | do |
| 14. | do not | do |
| 15. | do | do not |
| 16. | do not | do |
| 17. | do | do not |
| 18. | do | do not |
| 19. | do | do not |
| 20. | do not | do |

Score of 0 to 10: You possess clear traditional gender role beliefs. You have been socialized to believe in traditional gender roles. With the changing times, we must learn to question traditional gender roles and their effects on each gender. Do these traditional gender roles discriminate against males or females? Do they give males or females an advantage? How can we work to reduce the amount of gender bias present in our society to give both males and females equal opportunities, responsibilities, and chances for success?

Score of 11 to 15: This score is likely to be most common among self-assessors. Many individuals have grown up learning to accept that men and women have different responsibilities and abilities. Yet throughout our lives, we start to question gender roles as we interact with both men and women, all with unique characteristics, talents, skills, responsibilities, successes, and duties. As society continues to move toward gender equality, we must also shift our belief system to accept its shift. Gender bias is hindering our society's progress!

Score of 16 to 20: Although inevitably socialized by society to accept traditional gender role beliefs, you have been able to navigate around the serious gender role socialization present in our society. Keep working to promote gender equality in the workplace and in society!

# What We Can Do to Stop Gender Inequality?

1. Stand up for an individual when we feel he or she is being discriminated against based on his or her gender.
2. Work with our spouses to develop active parenting and share responsibilities in the home.
3. Generate awareness among parents and children about the harmful effects of gender socialization in our society.
4. Work to eliminate harmful language used to identify or objectify the opposite sex (e.g., "whore," "slut," "bitch," "Man up!" "Grow a pair!" "prude," "wearing the pants in the relationship," "like a girl"). Remember that these phrases, although they might seem harmless, can damage an individual's self-image.
5. Encourage the children in our lives to play as they wish. If they want to play with dolls, encourage this behavior. If they want to play with action figures, encourage this behavior.
6. Stand up to street harassment. As a bystander or as a victim, don't be afraid to respond to street harassment! No more catcalling.
7. Include men and women in the conversation about gender equality. Advocate for change for ourselves and for others. "Both men and women should feel free to be sensitive. Both men and women should feel free to be strong. It is time that we all perceive gender on a spectrum, instead of two sets of opposing ideals. If we stop defining each other by what we are not and start defining ourselves by who we are, we can all be freer" (Emma Watson).
8. Use social media to bring attention to gender imbalances. Social media is a powerful tool that can spread awareness about the gender biases in our society.
9. Build an inclusive culture in our workplaces. People are more likely to stand up to issues such as harassment, bullying and gender-based violence if it is made clear that this type of discrimination is not tolerated in our work environments. We must foster a sense of team cohesion through team building activities and bonding after work to encourage inclusion among men and women.
10. Remain aware of our own language and actions around others. If we are conscious of how our behavior will affect others, we can work to become a more inclusive and less discriminatory society.

**FUN FACT** Research shows that women are most likely to be complimented or appreciated for their physical appearance, while men are most likely to be complimented or appreciated for their achievements.

# Section 3:
# Building A Healthy Lifestyle

# BUILDING HEALTHY LIFESTYLES

Establishing and maintaining healthy habits is imperative if we are to achieve wellness and happiness in our lives. A healthy lifestyle encompasses: following healthy dietary guidelines; refraining from abusing mind- or mood-altering substances; developing and nurturing healthy interpersonal relationships; being proactive in maintaining our mental, physical, and emotional well-being; practicing oral hygiene; being financially responsible; choosing a career that provides us with new challenges and opportunities for personal and professional growth; and being a life-long learner. In this section, you will assess your current lifestyle, identify areas for improvement, and identify actions you will take to help you make these improvements.

# Objectives

At the end of this section, the participant will be able to

1. identify ways that diet and exercise can improve your quality of life,
2. identify healthy dietary guidelines,
3. identify the health benefits of exercising,
4. identify the harmful effects of certain substances, and
5. verbalize a clear understanding of how these harmful substances negatively affect your life.

# DIET AND EXERCISE

The following information was obtained directly from the Harvard School of Public Health, the American Heart Association (AHA), the Center of Nutrition Policy and Promotion (CNPP), the National Institute of Health (NIH), and the Centers for Disease Control and Prevention (CDC).

• Obesity is defined by the Mayo Clinic as a complex disorder involving an excessive amount of fat for a particular height from fat, muscle, bone, water, or a combination of these factors. Being overweight and obese are the result of "caloric imbalance"—too few calories burned for the amount of calories consumed—and are affected by various genetic, behavioral, and environmental factors. Obesity is a serious and prevalent issue in the United States, among children and adults.

• Being overweight or obese is not a cosmetic problem. These conditions greatly elevate your risk for other health conditions, including high blood pressure, coronary heart disease, type 2 diabetes, stroke, high blood cholesterol, metabolic syndrome, osteoarthritis, sleep apnea, cancer, obesity hypoventilation syndrome, reproductive problems, gallstones, asthma, bone and joint problems, and gout. Being overweight or obese also leads to a range of psychological issues.

• According to the National Institute of Health's research on obesity, childhood obesity has "more than doubled in children and quadrupled in adolescents in the past thirty years. In 2012, more than one third of children and adolescents were overweight or obese". Many influences within our society have a considerable effect on the dietary and exercise behaviors of children. Families, schools and childcare settings, the media, community welfare, and the food, beverage, and entertainment industries all take part in establishing the tendencies of our youth in their healthy (or unhealthy) lifestyles. To prevent obesity in children and adolescents, healthy habits must start at an early age and perpetuated by parents and role models.

• More than one-third of American adults are obese. The United States spent $147 billion in 2008 on medical costs for obese individuals, an estimated $1,429 higher per person than those of normal weight. Obesity is more common amongst middle-age adults, (40–59 years old), than among younger adults (20–39 years old).

## What Can We Do?

Although popular media stresses the importance of and advertises for the newest breakthrough "miracle" diet, the best way to maintain your weight and thus prevent obesity is easy: keep it simple. Stop with the Atkins diet, the South Beach diet, the tummy tuck surgeries, and Nutrisystem. In other words, eating healthy foods and exercising are the best way to maintain a healthy body. Again, *keep it simple!*

There are certain nutrients and foods that our bodies need in order to survive, grow, and flourish (e.g., fruits, vegetables, grains). Then there are the nutrients and foods that our bodies want because they taste good (e.g., fast food, french fries, brownies, doughnuts, potato chips, soda, etc.). But these foods we so desperately want are not the foods that our bodies need, and that difference between wants and needs could be the difference between a healthy, normal weighted body and a sluggish, overweight body.

# DIETARY GUIDELINES

- To establish and maintain good health, eat foods rich in protein, vitamins, minerals, and fiber.

- Engaging in physical activity serves to maintain or improve your weight and reduce your chances of having high blood pressure, heart disease, stroke, certain cancers, and diabetes.

- Opt for a diet with plenty of grain products, vegetables, and fruits, which can help you lower your intake of fat.

- To reduce your risk of heart attack and certain types of cancer, choose a diet low in fat, saturated fat, and cholesterol. (How do I know what foods are low in fat, saturated fat, and cholesterol? Read the label! All nutrition facts about a food must be on its label by law.)

- Watch your sugar intake! (The World Health Organization has stated that a person must not exceed 36 grams of sugar in a 24-hour period.)

- Watch your salt and sodium intake to minimize your risk of high blood pressure.

- Drink alcoholic beverages in moderation. Alcohol contains calories but little or no nutrients. Alcohol abuse is the cause of many health problems and can lead to addiction.

On the next page, you will find the food guide pyramid. It is an outline of what to eat each day. It is not a rigid prescription but a general guide that lets you choose a healthful diet that is right for you. Most Americans' diets are too high in fat and sodium. Thus, they should be minimized in a healthy diet. There are five major food groups shown in the three lower sections of the pyramid. Each of these food groups provides some, but not all, of the nutrients you need. Foods in one group can't replace those in another. No food group is more important than another. For good health, we need them all.

# The Food Guide Pyramid: What to Eat and How to Frequently Eat It

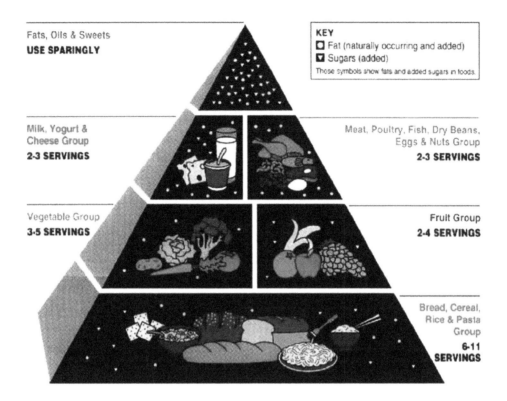

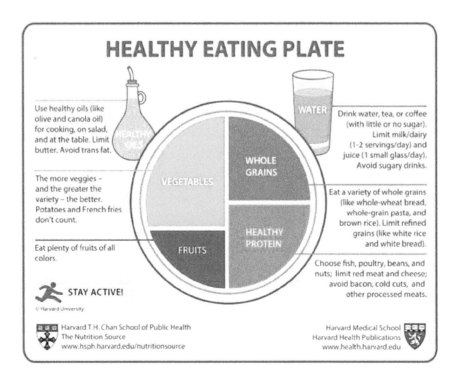

# WHAT IS A SERVING?

First off, the use of the word *serving* on the food pyramid is meant as a general guide. There is no need to measure servings when eating. But here is an easier way to picture it:

## Food Groups

**Carbohydrates:**

1 slice of bread
1 ounce of ready-to-eat cereal
½ cup of cooked cereal, rice, or pasta

**Vegetables:**

1 cup of raw leafy vegetables
½ cup of other vegetables, cooked or chopped raw
¾ cup of vegetable juice

**Fruits:**

1 medium apple, banana, or orange
½ cup of chopped, cooked, or canned fruit
¾ cup of fruit juice

**Dairy:**

1 cup of milk or yogurt
1½ ounces of natural cheese or 2 ounces of processed cheese

**Protein:**

2–3 ounces of cooked lean meat, poultry, or fish
½ cup of cooked dry beans or 1 egg (counts as 1 ounce of lean meat)
2 tablespoons of peanut butter or $\frac{1}{3}$ cup of nuts (counts as 1 ounce of lean meat)

***For more information on how to maintain a healthy and complete diet, go online to http://www.cnpp.usda.gov/sites/default/files/archived_projects/FGPPamphlet.pdf (or Google "The Food Guide Pyramid"), where you can find a complete pamphlet on the details of a healthy diet and lifestyle.

# READING LABELS

The following information was obtained directly from the Food and Drug Administration (FDA), the American Heart Association (AHA), and the American Diabetes Association (ADA).

Reading nutrition labels before ingesting any beverage, food, vitamin, or supplement is important if you want to attain and maintain a healthy body. We learned how to translate "the language of labels," and developed this section to pass this knowledge on to you, so that you too can make better decisions about what you buy and consume.

## Serving Size and Caloric Intake

"Nutrition Facts" labels identify the serving size and the number of servings in the package. Servings are given in familiar units, such as cups or pieces, which will tell you the size of a single serving and the number of servings in each package.

Caution! It is important to note the serving size, then ask yourself, "How many servings am I consuming?" (½ serving, 1 serving, or more?). For foods such as potato chips, the company may advertise "Only 150 calories!" but most of the time, this amount means 150 calories per serving. In the average bag of potato chips, there may be five or six servings, which equates to the entire bag being about 750 to 900 calories!

Within a healthy, balanced diet, the average person needs between 2,000 and 2,500 calories a day to maintain current weight. Eating foods high in calories, such as potato chips, fried chicken, macaroni and cheese, and doughnuts, makes it very difficult to remain within the caloric intake guidelines. When individuals consistently exceed their recommended calorie intake, weight gain becomes inevitable. To lose weight, simply eat fewer calories than your body burns. To maintain weight, eat about the same amount of calories that your body burns.

## Saturated Fat

We obtain saturated fat from red meat, whole milk, cheese, coconut oil, and many baked goods. An excessive amount of saturated fats in the diet can drive up cholesterol,

Want an extra push the next time you exercise? Reach for dark chocolate. A new study from the Journal of the International Society of Sports Nutrition found that cyclists who ate 40g of dark chocolate each day were able to ride 17% farther than those who didn't. Try it now! Replace one daily snack with 1 ½ squares of dark chocolate. Any bar with at least 70% cacao will do the trick

which increases the risk of heart disease and stroke. Most nutritionists suggest reducing saturated fat to under 10% of calories per day.

## Trans Fat

Trans fats have no known health benefits. Also known as partially hydrogenated oil, trans fat is the most harmful of dietary fats. Common sources of trans fat include doughnuts, cookies, crackers, muffins, fried foods, pies and cakes (and all other junk foods we crave from time to time!). Eating foods rich in trans fat increases the amount of harmful cholesterol in the bloodstream and reduces the amount of beneficial cholesterol. They create inflammation, which is linked to heart disease, stroke, diabetes, and other chronic conditions.

## Sodium

(Refer to the "Sodium" Fact Sheet.)

Sounds like we have to cut out a lot of food! Are there any foods that we should eat more of? Yes. The FDA and AHA both suggest that increasing the intake of dietary fiber, protein, calcium, iron, vitamins, and other nutrients is beneficial to a healthy diet and body. Let's take a look at these.

## Fiber

This plant-based nutrient has many benefits. It is recommended that we consume 25 to 30 grams per day. Fiber decreases the rate at which sugar is absorbed into the bloodstream, which keeps blood glucose levels from rising too quickly. This process allows us to stay full far longer and prevents overeating. Fiber also assists in maintaining a healthy digestive system. Fiber cleans our colon from bacteria and reduces our risk for colon cancer. It can be found in food items such as whole grain breads, cereals, brown rice, beans and legumes, fruits, and vegetables.

## Protein

The human diet actually requires substantial amounts of protein in order to maintain health. Protein is involved in every cell in our body; even our hair and nails are

Not so healthy: flavored yogurt can pack 35 grams of sugar into each cup! Instead, select plain Greek yogurt and top it with nuts and berries. You'll get more protein and fiber for a sustained energy boost.

mostly made up of protein. Our bodies use protein to build and restore tissue, as well as to make enzymes, hormones, and other body chemicals. Protein is also an important building block of bones, muscles, skin, cartilage, and blood. A diet with a lack of protein can put our body's equilibrium out of whack, causing many different health issues. Protein comes from a variety of sources, including meat, milk, fish, soy, and eggs, as well as beans, legumes, and nut butters (peanut butter, almond butter, cashew butter, etc.).

It is recommended that men consume 56 grams and that women consume 46 grams of protein every day.

## Calcium

This nutrient is a vital mineral necessary for bone health and age-defying beauty. Even though our bodies need calcium, we do not produce the mineral internally. We get it from the foods we eat every day. Yet, most people do not have enough calcium in their diets. Common sources of calcium include milk, vegetables (collards, okra, spinach, turnip greens), yogurt, cheese, and fish. A lack of calcium can lead to osteoporosis, a disease where our bones become fragile and break easily.

## Iron

The most common nutrient deficiency in our nation is iron deficiency. Many women experience it due to loss of blood during menstruation and pregnancy. Iron deficiency can lead to anemia, which causes tiredness, dizziness, and other harmful effects. Common sources of iron include pork, red meat, seafood, poultry, dried fruit, beans, and dark green leafy vegetables.

## Percentage of Daily Value

The % Daily Value (DV) reveals to us the percentage of each nutrient in a serving, in terms of the daily recommended amount. The percentage DV is found on the right column of the "Nutrition Facts" label, next to each nutrient that is included in the food item. If you wish to consume less of a certain nutrient (such as saturated fat or sodium), choose foods with a DV of 5% or less. If you wish to consume more of a nutrient (such as fiber), look for foods with a DV of 20% or more. We must remember that the percentage DVs are based on 2,000 calories per day. Depending on your own characteristics and goals, you may need to consume less or more than 2,000 calories per day.

# Nutrition Facts

**1**

Serving Size 2/3 cup (55g)
Servings Per Container About 8

**2**

**Amount Per Serving**

**Calories** 230          Calories from Fat 40

**% Daily Value***

| | |
|---|---|
| **Total Fat** 8g | **12%** |
| Saturated Fat 1g | **5%** |
| *Trans* Fat 0g | |
| **Cholesterol** 0mg | **0%** |
| **Sodium** 160mg | **7%** |
| **Total Carbohydrate** 37g | **12%** |
| Dietary Fiber 4g | **16%** |
| Sugars 1g | |
| **Protein** 3g | |

**3**

**4**

| | |
|---|---|
| Vitamin A | 10% |
| Vitamin C | 8% |
| Calcium | 20% |
| Iron | 45% |

* Percent Daily Values are based on a 2,000 calorie diet.
  Your daily value may be higher or lower depending on
  your calorie needs.

**5**

| | Calories: | 2,000 | 2,500 |
|---|---|---|---|
| Total Fat | Less than | 65g | 80g |
| Sat Fat | Less than | 20g | 25g |
| Cholesterol | Less than | 300mg | 300mg |
| Sodium | Less than | 2,400mg | 2,400mg |
| Total Carbohydrate | | 300g | 375g |
| Dietary Fiber | | 25g | 30g |

# Exercise

Along with a balanced diet, exercise is imperative in keeping our bodies healthy. What are the benefits of regular physical activity?

Exercise controls weight. Exercise can help to inhibit weight gain or help to sustain weight loss. When we exercise, we burn calories. The more intense the activity, the more calories we burn. Setting aside large chunks of time for exercise isn't necessary to reap weight-loss benefits. If you are unable to go to the gym or workout at home, get more active throughout the day in simple ways—take the stairs instead of the elevator, intensify household chores, park your car farther away from shops and work.

✔ Exercise combats health issues and disease. Being active keeps your blood flowing steadily, which decreases risk of cardiovascular diseases. In fact, regular physical activity can help prevent or reduce the effects of a number of health issues, including stroke, type 2 diabetes, depression, cancer, and arthritis.

✔ Exercise lifts our mood. It stimulates certain brain chemicals that make us feel happier and less stressed. Exercising regularly can make us feel better about our own appearance, improving our self-image.

✔ Exercise boosts energy. Frequent physical activity can develop our muscle strength and improve endurance. Working out sends nutrients and oxygen to our tissues, helping our cardiovascular system work more efficiently. And when our heart and lungs work more efficiently, we have more energy throughout the day.

✔ Exercise stimulates better sleep. Regular physical activity means falling asleep faster and deepening sleep.

✔ Exercise can be fun! Physical activity is a fun way to spend time alone or with others. It provides us with an opportunity to unwind, spend time outside, or simply become involved in activities that bring us joy. Exercise can also help us connect with family or friends. So take a yoga class, go for a hike with friends, or join a soccer team. Find a physical activity you love and *go for it*! Whatever you try, you will be prolonging your life and maintaining a healthy lifestyle.

# The Major Health Benefits of Walking
Source: *Prevention Magazine*, January 2015

### Bones
4 hours a week can reduce the risk of hip fractures by up to 43%.

### Brain
2 hours of walking a week can reduce risk of stroke by 30%.

### Health
Logging 3,500 steps a day lowers risk of diabetes by 29%.

### Heart
30 to 60 minutes most days of the week drastically lowers risk of heart disease.

### Longevity
75 minutes a week of brisk walking can add almost 2 years to our lives.

### Memory
40 minutes, 3 times a week, protects that part of our brain region associated with planning and memory.

### Mood
30 minutes a day can reduce symptoms of depression by 36%.

### Weight
A daily 60-minute walk can cut the risk of obesity in half.

A full 68% of packaged foods contain added sweeteners, which can be tricky to spot because they are hidden behind ingredients listed under names like evaporated cane juice.

# How Am I Doing?

Please answer each question honestly and with as much detail as possible. Remember, the questions are designed to help you understand your lifestyle as it relates to your health and well-being. If the question does not pertain to your lifestyle, please explain what a negative impact a lack of a healthy diet and exercise would have on your life.

In the past, a lack of diet and exercise has negatively impacted my . . .

_____

_____

_____

Health

_____

_____

_____

Finances

_____

_____

_____

Social relationships

_____

_____

_____

Professional paths

_____

_____

_____

# Sodium

This information was obtained from the
National Institutes of Health, the US Library of Medicine, the
New York Times Health Guide, and the Mayo Clinic.

Sodium is an element that the body needs to work properly. The most common form of sodium is sodium chloride, which is table salt. Naturally, milk, beets, drinking water, and celery contain sodium. High levels of sodium are found in Worcestershire sauce, soy sauce, soups, onion salt, and garlic salt. American dietary habits often include large amounts of sodium, even if we do not add it intentionally.

Sodium is necessary to control blood pressure and blood volume. The body also needs sodium for nerves and muscles to function properly. Most people are consuming far more sodium than is recommended, which could lead to serious health problems.

Consider this: a single teaspoon of table salt has 2,325 milligrams of sodium, which the DASH (Dietary Approaches to Stop Hypertension) diet says is twice the recommended daily intake. Most nutritionists recommend limiting sodium intake to less than 2,300 milligrams per day. (Most Americans are thought to consume about 3,400 milligrams of sodium daily.)

When we consume too much sodium, it starts to accumulate in our blood, causing blood volume to increase. The heart must work harder on the increased blood volume, which increases the pressure in our arteries. Chronic buildup of sodium leads to high blood pressure and perhaps eventually may cause congestive heart failure, chronic kidney disease, and cirrhosis of the liver.

The Mayo Clinic recommends that "adults who have high blood pressure should have no more than 1,500 milligrams of sodium in a 24-hour period". Individuals with congestive heart failure, cirrhosis of the liver, and/or kidney disease may require much lower amounts. So how can we avoid these conditions and still enjoy our food? Here are some suggestions.

Eat fresh foods. Most "fresh" fruits, vegetables, and meats are naturally low in sodium. Unfortunately, some of our favorite foods (e.g., lunch meat, bacon, hot dogs, sausage, and ham) have high levels of sodium. It is important to buy fresh or frozen poultry or meat that hasn't been injected with a sodium-containing solution. (Here is another time when reading the label is particularly important!)

Reduce or remove salt from recipes, whenever possible. Many dishes taste just as good with reduced salt. There are many cookbooks on the market that focus on reducing health risks and encouraging healthy dishes.

Limit use of condiments overloaded with sodium. Many sauces, dips, ketchup, mustard, and relish contain large amounts of nonessential sodium. Think about the daily recommended intake of sodium before buying these condiments at the store.

Utilize sodium alternatives. Herbs, spices and juice from citrus fruit offer healthier options with much less sodium. Consider using these alternatives in your recipes to achieve the same taste and ensure healthier meals. Despite popular misconceptions, sea salt is not a good substitute. It has about the same amount of sodium as table salt.

People who get morning sunlight have significantly lower Body Mass Indexes (BMIs) than those who get exposure later in the day. A 20- to 30-minute walk before noon is suggested.

# Salt Substitutes

The market today has a number of salt substitutes; however, many of them contain potassium chloride, which is harmful if you have kidney problems or if you take medication for congestive heart failure or high blood pressure.

Taste alone may not tell you which foods are high in sodium. Take a bagel for example. While it may not taste salty, a typically-sized oat-bran bagel has about 600 milligrams of sodium. One slice of whole wheat bread contains about 100 milligrams of sodium.

So then how can we go about reducing our sodium intake? The Mayo Clinic suggests reading nutrition labels and limiting the purchase of products with the following ingredients: monosodium glutamate (MSG), baking soda (sodium bicarbonate), baking powder, disodium phosphate, sodium alginate, sodium citrate, and sodium nitrite

The sodium content listed on product labels can sometimes be very confusing. How can I better understand them? Here are the definitions that the FDA (Food and Drug Administration) has given to help us make sense of the sodium content on nutrition labels:

- Sodium-free or salt-free: each serving of this product contains less than 5 milligrams

- Very low sodium: each serving contains 35 milligrams of sodium or less

- Low sodium: each serving contains 140 milligrams of sodium or less

- Reduced or low sodium: the product contains at least 25% less sodium

- Lite or light in sodium: sodium has been reduced by at least 50%

- Unsalted or no salt added: no salt added during processing of the food. However, other ingredients may be high in sodium.

The 5-second rule. Ever drop food on the floor, then eat it if it met the 5-second rule? The worst case scenario is that you could get a foodborne illness, but that is highly unlikely, unless you have a very dirty floor.

# How Am I Doing?

Please answer each question honestly and with as much detail as possible. Remember, the questions are designed to help you understand your lifestyle as it relates to your health and well-being. If the question does not pertain to your lifestyle, please explain what a negative impact the sodium would have on your life if you did consume them regularly.

In the past, the consumption of sodium has negatively impacted my . . .

Health

_____

_____

_____

It is important that I work on reducing my sodium intake because . . .

_____

_____

_____

# Energy Drinks and Caffeine

The following information was obtained from the National Institute of Health (NIH), the Centers for Disease Control and Prevention (CDC), the Mayo Clinic, and the University of California Department of Agriculture and Natural Resources (ANR).

Energy drinks are beverages that contain caffeine in combination with other harmful ingredients such as taurine, guarana, and B vitamins. They are popularly promoted as products that boost energy and enhance physical as well as mental ability. The energy drink is the most widespread dietary supplement consumed by America's young adults, next to multivitamins.

Males, aged 18 to 34 years, consume the greatest number of energy drinks out of any age group. Nearly one-third of teens between 12 and 17 years of age drink them regularly.

Caffeine is the main ingredient in almost all energy drinks. The amount of caffeine in four or five cups of coffee can be found in one 24-ounce energy drink (as much as 500 milligrams of caffeine!) Energy drinks oftentimes contain guarana, which is an additional source of caffeine sometimes called Brazilian cocoa. Adding in the guarana as an extra source of caffeine opens up the possibility for more serious health concerns, as too much caffeine in a short amount of time can be extremely harmful to the body. Most energy drinks can have as high as 294 milligrams of caffeine in a single 8- to 12-fluid-ounce bottle.

## Health Risks

According to the National Institute of Health, the total number of visits to the emergency room related directly to energy drink issues doubled between 2007 and 2011. Increasingly, we see a trend emerging among young adults to mix energy drinks with alcohol. The 25% of college students who consume alcohol with energy drinks tend to binge drink at a significantly higher rate than those who do not mix the two beverages. In 2011, "42% of all energy-drink related emergency room visits involved combining beverages with alcohol or drugs (including illicit drugs like marijuana, as well as central nervous system stimulants, like Ritalin or Adderall)", according to the NIH.

Those who consume alcohol with energy drinks triple their chances of binge drinking when compared to those who do not mix alcohol and energy drinks.

Research shows that too much caffeine can lead to issues with heart rhythm, blood flow, and blood pressure. Additionally, caffeine can seriously damage the developing cardiovascular and nervous systems of children. Caffeine use in excess, which is more common among American adults than many think, is linked with anxiety, digestive issues, heightened blood pressure, dehydration, sleep problems, and palpitations.

Young adults who mix alcohol with caffeinated beverages are less capable of determining how intoxicated they've become, which places them at greater risk for binge drinking, unconsciousness, or even death. When alcohol is mixed with energy drinks, the caffeine in these drinks can disguise the sedative, or depressant, effects of alcohol. Meanwhile, caffeine does not have any effect on the breaking down of alcohol by the liver. Thus, caffeine does not at all lessen breath alcohol concentrations or minimize the risk of alcohol-related injuries or damages.

According to the CDC, "drinkers who consume alcohol with energy drinks are about twice as likely as drinkers who do not report mixing alcohol with energy drinks to report being taken advantage of sexually, taking advantage of someone else sexually, and riding with a driver who is under the influence of alcohol."

Consuming too many energy drinks can interfere with young adults' sleep patterns and increase their impulsivity and risk-taking behaviors.

- Energy drink consumption may cause serious fat increase and weight gain, since many energy drinks contain as much as 25-50 grams of sugar. The high sugar content can be especially problematic for those who are diabetic or have other related health conditions.
- Energy drinks give the consumer massive doses of caffeine and other artificial supplements that stimulate and energize your system, for a short period of time. Drinking energy drinks daily can mislead the consumer into thinking they cannot operate without it. This is, when people become dependent on energy drinks to get them through their day.
- Energy drinks have no regulations to guarantee that they accurately mark the actual caffeine content on the label of each drink.

## Misconceptions on the Drinks' Effectiveness

There is very little data to support the belief that caffeinated energy drinks actually improve alertness and physical endurance. According to the US Food and Drug Administration (FDA), there is limited evidence to prove that drinking energy drinks can significantly improve physical and mental performance, enhance driving ability when tired, or decrease mental fatigue during long periods of concentration. Unfortunately, the collection of literature on the subject is limited, and more research is necessary to fully understand the harmful effects of energy drinks and their effectiveness.

## Caffeinated Alcoholic Beverages

According to the Centers for Disease Control, caffeinated alcoholic beverages (CABs) are "premixed beverages that combine alcohol, caffeine, and other stimulants". They tend to have higher alcohol content than beer; most CABs have 5%-12% alcohol content, whereas most beers have 4%-5%. Yet, the caffeine content in these beverages is seldom reported. After being introduced into the marketplace, CABs experienced a sudden increase in popularity. Manufacturers promoting their CAB products marketed them heavily among young people, pushing youth-oriented graphic images and messages.

---

Have you ever heard the phrase "everything in moderation"? It rings true for every nutrient, food, beverage, and supplement you ingest into your body. Anything in excess is unhealthy. Even too much water can cause strain on your organs and even possibly death. Please think carefully about what you are putting into your body!

---

# How Am I Doing?

Please answer each question honestly and with as much detail as possible. Remember, the questions are designed to help you understand your lifestyle as it relates to your health and well-being. If the question does not pertain to your lifestyle, please explain what a negative impact the substances would have on your life if you did consume them regularly.

In the past, my consumption of energy drinks or caffeine has negatively impacted my . . .

Health

_____

_____

_____

Finances

_____

_____

_____

Social relationships

_____

_____

_____

Professional paths

_____

_____

_____

It is important to reduce my consumption of energy drinks and caffeine, because . . .

_____

_____

_____

# Alcohol (ethyl alcohol)

The following information was obtained directly from the National Institute on Alcohol Abuse and Alcoholism (NIAAA), National Institute on Drug Abuse (NIDA), Centers for Disease Control and Prevention (CDC), and the Substance Abuse and Mental Health Services Administration (SAMHSA).

Low risk drinking is defined by NIAAA as: women—no more than 3 drinks on any single day, and no more than 7 drinks per week; men—no more than 4 drinks on any single day, and no more than 14 drinks per week.

Heavy drinking is defined by SAMHSA as "drinking 5 or more drinks in the same occasion on each of 5 or more days in the past 30 days."

Binge drinking is the most common pattern of excessive alcohol use in the United States. The NIAAA and SAMHSA define binge drinking as "a pattern of drinking that brings a person's blood alcohol concentration (BAC) to 0.08 grams percent or above. This typically happens when men consume 5 or more drinks, and when women consume 4 or more drinks, in about 2 hours." According to the Centers for Disease Control and Prevention,

- 1 in 6 US adults drink about four times a month, consuming 8 drinks per binge
- Binge drinking is more common among adults aged 18–34, but drinkers aged 65 and older report binge drinking more often—an average of five to six times a month
- Binge drinking is more common among those with household incomes of $75,000 or more than among those with lower incomes
- Approximately 92% of US adults who drink excessively report binge drinking in the past 30 days
- Although college students commonly binge drink (37.9%), 70% of binge drinking episodes involve adults age 26 and older
- The prevalence of binge drinking among men is twice the prevalence among women
- Binge drinkers are fourteen times more likely to report alcohol-impaired driving than non–binge drinkers
- About 90% of the alcohol consumed by youth under the age of 21 in the USA is in the form of binge drinks

- More than half of the alcohol consumed by all adults in the USA aged 21 and older is in the form of binge drinks

Binge drinking is associated with many health problems, including the following:
- accidental injuries (e.g., falls, car crashes, drowning, burns)
- intentional injuries (e.g., firearms, domestic violence, sexual assault)
- liver disease
- poor control of diabetes
- unintentional pregnancy
- alcohol poisoning
- children born with fetal alcohol spectrum disorders
- neurological damage
- high blood pressure, stroke, and other cardiovascular conditions
- sexual dysfunction
- sexually transmitted diseases

**The following information was obtained from the National Institute of Health's "Alcohol Facts and Statistics" study.**

Alcohol abuse cost the USA $249 billion in 2010 (or $2.05 per drink), in the form of lost productivity, health care costs, criminal activity, and other expenses. Binge drinking was responsible for 77% of these costs, or $191 billion.

There were 16.3 million American adults aged 18 and older who had an alcohol use disorder (AUD) in 2014 (10.6 million men and 5.7 million women). About 1.5 million adults sought treatment for an AUD in 2014, which represents about 8.9% of adults who reportedly needed treatment. Men who received treatment (1.1 million) in 2014 were almost three times the number of women who received treatment (431,000).

In 2014, in the USA, an estimated 679,000 adolescents aged 12–17 had an AUD (367,000 females and 312,000 males). An estimated 55,000 adolescents (18,000 males and 37,000 females) received treatment for an AUD in 2014.

Nearly 88,000 people (about 62,000 men and 26,000 women) die each year in the USA from alcohol-related causes, making alcohol the fourth leading cause of preventable death in the USA. In 2014, alcohol-impaired driving fatalities accounted for 9,967 deaths

(31% of overall driving fatalities).

More than 10% of children residing in the USA have at least one parent with an alcohol-related problem (2012 study). The 2014 National Survey on Drug Use and Health (NSDUH) found that 34.7% of 15-year-olds reported having at least one drink in their lives. About 8.7 million people aged 12–20 (22.8% of this age group) reported drinking alcohol in the past month (23% males and 22.5% females).

The National Institute on Alcohol Abuse and Alcoholism contends that alcohol use during adolescence inhibits normal brain development for youths and increases the chance of developing an alcohol use disorder. In addition, underage drinking leads to a wide range of serious consequences, including sexual assault, injuries, and even deaths—including those from car accidents. The following information was obtained directly from the Substance Abuse and Mental Health Services Administration to demonstrate the issues faced on college campuses pertaining to alcohol.

---

It is estimated that each year, on American college campuses:
- 1,825 college students between the ages of 18 and 24 die from alcohol-related, unintentional injuries, including motor vehicle crashes.
- 696,000 students between the ages of 18 and 24 are assaulted (physically attacked without provocation) by another student who has been drinking.
- 97,000 students between the ages of 18 and 24 report experiencing alcohol-related sexual assault or date rape (it is believed that only 1 in 4 sexual assaults and rapes are reported).
- Roughly 20% of college students meet the criteria for an alcohol use disorder.
- About 1 in 4 college students report academic consequences from drinking (e.g., missing classes, falling behind in class, doing poorly on examinations or papers, receiving lower grades overall, and dropping out of school).

The World Health Organization states that 2012 saw approximately 3.3 million deaths that could be linked to alcohol consumption. Worldwide, alcohol abuse is the "first leading risk factor for death and disability among persons in the age group 20–39", and it is the "fifth leading risk factor among people between the ages of 15 and 49".

# The Human Body

- Brain—Alcohol interferes with the brain's communication paths, causing changes in mood/behavior and making it more difficult to think clearly and to move with coordination.

- Heart—Heavy drinking over a long period of time, or binge drinking over a short period of time, can harm the heart, leading to issues such as cardiomyopathy (stretching and drooping of the heart muscle), arrhythmias (irregular heart beat), stroke, and high blood pressure.

- Liver—Heavy drinking has been identified as a leading cause of steatosis (fatty liver), alcohol hepatitis, fibrosis, or cirrhosis. In 2013, of the 72,559 liver disease deaths among individuals aged 12 and older, 45.8% involved alcohol (48.5% of males and 41.8% of females). Among all cirrhosis deaths in 2011, 48% were alcohol-related. In 2009, alcohol-related liver disease was the primary cause of almost 1 in 3 liver transplants in the USA (American Board of Addiction Medicine).

- Pancreas—Consuming alcohol signals the pancreas to produce toxic substances that eventually cause pancreatitis, a severe inflammation of the blood vessels in the pancreas that prevents healthy digestion.

- Cancer—Excessive consumption of alcohol increases the risk of contracting certain cancers, including cancers of the mouth, esophagus, throat, liver, and breast.

- Immune system——Drinking too much alcohol weakens the body's immune system, making it susceptible to disease. Chronic drinkers are more likely to contract diseases, like pneumonia and tuberculosis, than people who abuse alcohol. Drinking a lot in a single occasion significantly restricts the body's ability to fight off infections.

# How Am I Doing?

Please answer each question honestly and with as much detail as possible. Remember, the questions are designed to help you understand your lifestyle as it relates to your health and well-being.

In the past, the consumption of alcohol has negatively impacted my . . .

Health

_____

_____

_____

Finances

_____

_____

_____

Social relationships

_____

_____

_____

Professional paths

_____

_____

_____

It is important to closely monitor my consumption of alcohol, because . . .

_____

_____

_____

King Louis XIV of France established in his court the position of "Royal Chocolate Maker to the King".

# Commonly Known Drugs

The purpose of this exercise is to provide you with factual information about the most commonly known drugs, what they are known by, their commercial uses, the short- and long-term effects on the body and brain, co-occurring mental health issues, how the drugs interact with ethyl alcohol, and what occurs when an individual withdraws from the substance. Sources of information were the National Institutes of Health (NIH), National Institute on Alcohol Abuse and Alcoholism (NIAAA), the National Institute on Drug Abuse (NIDA), the Centers for Disease Control and Prevention (CDC), and the Substance Abuse and Mental Health Services Administration (SAMHSA).

## *Cannabis sativa* (Marijuana)

Made from the hemp plant, *Cannabis sativa*. The main psychoactive (mind-altering) chemical in marijuana is delta-9-tetrahydrocannabinol (THC). Street names—blunt, bud, ganja, grass, joint, pot, reefer, smoke, weed, hashish. Commercial uses—none known.

Short-term effects: Enhanced sensory perception and euphoria followed by drowsiness or relaxation, slowed reaction time, problems with balance and coordination, increased heart rate, increased appetite, problems with learning and memory.

Long-term effects: Frequent respiratory infections.

Other health issues: Youth—impaired short- and long-term memory. Pregnant women—babies are born with problems related to attention, memory, and problem-solving.

Mental health issues: Depression, anxiety, mood swings, paranoia.

In combination with alcohol: Increased heart rate and blood pressure, further slowing of mental processing and reaction time.

Withdrawal symptoms: Irritability, trouble sleeping, decreased appetite, anxiety, increased blood pressure, abdominal pain and nausea, euphoria, increased energy, alertness, insomnia, headaches, restlessness, heart rhythm problems, heart attack, stroke, seizure, coma.

# Cocaine

Cocaine is a powerful stimulant drug made from the leaves of the coca plant, which is native to South America. Street names—blow, coke, crack, rock. Commercial uses—hydrochloride topical solution (anesthetic rarely used in medical procedures).

Short-term effects: Narrowed blood vessels, enlarged pupils, increased body temperature, increased heart rate and blood pressure, abdominal pain and nausea, euphoria, increased energy, alertness, insomnia, headaches, restlessness, heart rhythm problems, heart attack, stroke, seizure, coma.

Long-term effects: Loss of sense of smell, nosebleeds, nasal damage and trouble swallowing from snorting, infection and death of bowel tissue from decreased blood flow, poor nutrition, and weight loss from decreased appetite.

*Danger: Overdose may cause permanent brain damage, coma, or death.*

Other health issues: Pregnant women—premature delivery, low birth weight, neonatal abstinence syndrome, risk of HIV, hepatitis, and other infectious diseases from shared needles.

Mental health issues: Anxiety, panic attacks, paranoia, erratic and violent behavior, psychosis.

In combination with alcohol: Increased risk of overdose and sudden death than from either drug being taken alone.

Withdrawal symptoms: Depression, tiredness, increased appetite, insomnia, vivid, unpleasant dreams, slowed thinking and movement, restlessness.

# Dextromethorphan, or DXM
# (Over-the-counter cough/cold medicines)

Psychoactive when taken in higher-than-recommended amounts. Street names—robo, triple C. Commercial uses—many brand names include "DM."

Short-term effects: Euphoria, slurred speech, increased heart rate and blood pressure, increased temperature, numbness, dizziness, nausea, vomiting, confusion, altered visual perceptions, and buildup of excess acid in body fluids.

Long-term effects: Unknown.

Other health issues: Breathing problems, seizures, and increased heart rate occur from other ingredients in cough/cold medicine.

Mental health issues: Mental confusion, paranoia.

In combination with Alcohol. Increased risk of confusion, paranoia, high blood pressure

# Gamma-Hydroxybutyrate, or Sodium Oxybate (GHB)

A depressant approved for use in the treatment of narcolepsy, a disorder that causes daytime "sleep attacks." Street names—Georgia home boy, grievous bodily harm, liquid ecstasy, liquid X, soap. Commercial uses—Xyrem.

Short-term effects: Euphoria, drowsiness, nausea or vomiting, unconsciousness, seizures, slowed heart rate and breathing, lower body temperature, coma, death.

Long-term effects: Unknown.

Other health issues: Known to be used as a "date rape" drug.

Mental health issues: Anxiety, confusion, memory loss, hallucinations, aggressive behavior.

In combination with alcohol: Causes nausea, problems with breathing, greatly increased depressant effects.

Withdrawal symptom: Insomnia, anxiety, tremors, sweating, increased heart rate and blood pressure, psychotic thoughts.

# Heroin

An opioid drug made from morphine, a natural substance extracted from the seed-pod of the Asian opium poppy plant. Street names—brown sugar, china white, dope, H, horse, junk, smack, white horse. Commercial uses—none known.

Short-term effects: Euphoria, flushing of skin, dry mouth, heavy feeling in hands and feet, alternate wakeful/drowsy states, itching, nausea, vomiting, slowed breathing and heart rate.

Long-term effects: Collapsed veins, abscesses (swollen tissue with pus), infection of the lining and valves in the heart, constipation, stomach cramps, liver or kidney disease, pneumonia.

*Danger: Overdose may cause permanent brain damage, a coma, or death.*

Other health issues: Pregnancy—miscarriage, low birth weight, neonatal abstinence syndrome.

Mental health issues: Clouded thinking, paranoia, anxiety.

In combination with alcohol: Dangerous slowdown of heart rate and breathing, coma, death.

Withdrawal symptoms: Restlessness, muscle and bone pain, insomnia, diarrhea, vomiting, cold flashes with goose bumps ("cold turkey"), uncontrolled leg movement.

## Inhalants

Solvents, aerosols, and gases found in household products, such as spray paints, markers, glues, and cleaning fluids; also nitrites (e.g., amyl nitrite), which are prescription medications for chest pain. Street names—poppers, snappers, whippets, laughing gas. Commercial uses—paint thinner or remover, degreasers, dry-cleaning fluid, gasoline, lighter fluid, correction fluid, permanent markers, electronics cleaners and freeze sprays, glue, spray paint, hair or deodorant sprays, fabric protector sprays, aerosol computer cleaning products, vegetable oil sprays, butane lighters, propane tanks, whipped cream aerosol containers, refrigerant gases, ether, chloroform, halothane, nitrous oxide.

Short-term effects: Nausea, slurred speech, lack of coordination, euphoria, dizziness, drowsiness, disinhibition, lightheadedness, headaches, sudden sniffing death due to heart failure (from butane, propane, and other chemicals in aerosols), death from asphyxiation, suffocation, convulsions or seizures, coma, choking.

Long-term effects: Collapsed veins, abscesses (swollen tissue with pus), infection of the lining and valves in the heart, constipation, stomach cramps, liver or kidney disease, pneumonia.

*Danger: Overdose may cause permanent brain damage, a coma, or death.*

Other health issues: Pregnant women—low birth weight, bone problems, delayed behavioral development due to brain problems, altered metabolism, and body composition.

Mental health issues: Confusion, hallucinations/delusions, mood changes, lack of oxygen causes problems with thinking.

In combination with alcohol: Dangerously low blood pressure.

Withdrawal symptom: Causes nausea, loss of appetite, sweating, tics, problems sleeping.

# Ketamine

A dissociative drug used as an anesthetic in veterinary practice. Dissociative drugs are hallucinogens that cause the user to feel detached from reality. Street names—cat valium, K, special K, vitamin K. Commercial uses—Ketalar.

Short-term effects: Sedation, problems moving, to the point of being immobile, raised blood pressure, unconsciousness, slowed breathing that can lead to death.

Long-term effects: Ulcers and pain in the bladder, kidney problems, stomach pain.

*Danger: Overdose may cause permanent brain damage, a coma, or death.*

Other health issues: Sometimes used as a "date rape" drug; risk of HIV, hepatitis, and other infectious diseases from shared needles.

Mental health issues: Problems with attention, learning and memory, dreamlike states, hallucinations, confusion and problems speaking, impaired memory, depression.

In combination with alcohol: Greatly increases the risk of confusion, memory loss, immobility, unconsciousness, slowed breathing, dangerously high blood pressure.

Withdrawal symptom: Unknown.

# Khat (Pronounced "cot")

A shrub (*Catha edulis*) found in East Africa and southern Arabia. Contains the psychoactive chemicals cathinone and cathine. People from African and Arabian regions (up to an estimated 20 million people worldwide) have used khat for centuries as part of cultural tradition, and for its stimulant-like effects. Street names—Abyssinian tea, African salad, catha, chat, kat, cat. Commercial uses—none.

Short-term effects: Euphoria, increased alertness and arousal, increased blood pressure and heart rate, irritability, loss of appetite, insomnia.

Long-term effects: Tooth decay and gum disease, gastrointestinal disorders such as constipation, ulcers, stomach inflammation, increased risk of upper gastrointestinal tumors, cardiovascular disorders such as irregular heartbeat, decreased blood flow, and heart attack

*Danger: Overdose may cause permanent brain damage, a coma, or death.*

Other health issues: In rare cases associated with heavy use—psychotic reactions (fantastical beliefs that one has superior qualities such as fame, power and wealth).

Mental health issues: Depression, nightmares, inability to concentrate, irritability, delusions, hallucinations, paranoia.

In combination with alcohol: Unknown.

Withdrawal symptom: trembling, lack of energy.

## Lysergic Acid Diethylamide (LSD)

A hallucinogen manufactured from lysergic acid, which found in ergot, a fungus that grows on rye and other grains. Street names—acid, blotter, microdot, yellow sunshine. Commercial uses—none known.

Short-term effects: Raised blood pressure, heart rate, body temperature, dizziness and insomnia, loss of appetite, sweating, numbness, tremors, enlarged pupils.

Long-term effects: Frightening flashbacks (called hallucinogen persisting perception disorder), ongoing visual disturbances.

Other health issues: Unknown.

Mental health issues: Paranoia, rapid emotional swings, distortion of a person's ability to recognize reality, think rationally or communicate with others, disorganized thinking.

In combination with alcohol: May decrease the perceived effects of alcohol.

Withdrawal symptom: Unknown.

## 3,4-Methylenedioxy-Methamphetamine (MDMA)

A synthetic psychoactive drug that has similarities to both the stimulant amphetamine and the hallucinogen mescaline. Also known as ecstasy or molly. Street names—Adam, Eve, lover's speed, uppers. Commercial uses—none known.

Short-term effects: Lowered inhibition, enhanced sensory perception, sleep problems, increased heart rate and blood pressure, muscle tension, teeth clenching, nausea, blurred vision, faintness, chills or sweating, sharp rise in body temperature leading to liver, kidney, or heart failure and death.

Long-term effects: Problems with sleep, loss of appetite, less interest in sex.

Other health issues: Unknown.

Mental health issues: Depression, confusion, anxiety, impaired memory, aggression, impulsivity, impaired concentration.

In combination with alcohol: May increase the risk of cell and organ damage.

Withdrawal symptom: Fatigue, loss of appetite, depression, trouble concentrating.

## Mescaline (Peyote)

A hallucinogen that is found in disk-shaped "buttons" in the crown of several cacti, including peyote. Street names—buttons, cactus, mesc. Commercial uses—none known.

Short-term effects: Euphoria, increased body temperature, heart rate, blood pressure, sweating, problems with movement.

Long-term effects: Unknown.

Other health issues: None known.

Mental health issues: Hallucinations, anxiety, altered perceptions of reality, impaired concentration.

In combination with alcohol: May reduce the perceived effects of alcohol.

# Methamphetamine

An extremely addictive stimulant amphetamine drug. Street names—crank, chalk, crystal, ice, meth, speed. Commercial uses—Desoxyn.

Short-term effects: Increased wakefulness and physical activity, decreased appetite, increased breathing, increased heart rate and blood pressure, increased temperature, irregular heartbeat.

Long-term effects: Insomnia, weight loss, severe dental problems ("meth mouth"), intense itching leading to skin scores from scratching.

*Danger: Overdose may cause permanent brain damage, a coma, or death.*

Other health issues: Pregnant women—premature delivery, separation of the placenta from the uterus, low birth weight, lethargy, heart and brain problems; risk of HIV, hepatitis, and other infectious diseases from shared needles.

Mental health issues: Anxiety, confusion, depression, mood swings, violent behavior, paranoia, delusions, hallucinations.

In combination with alcohol: Masks the depression effect of alcohol, increasing risk of alcohol overdose, may increase blood pressure and jitters.

Withdrawal symptom: Depression, anxiety, tiredness.

# Phencyclidine (PCP)

A dissociative drug developed as an intravenous anesthetic that has been discontinued due to serious adverse effects. Dissociative drugs are hallucinogens that cause the user to feel detached from reality. Street names—angel dust; peace pill. Commercial uses—none known.

Short-term effects: Delusions, hallucinations, and paranoia, problem thinking, a sense of distance from one's environment; anxiety. Low doses—slight increase in breathing rate, increased blood pressure and heart rate, shallow breathing, facial redness and sweating, numbness of the hands or feet, problems with movement. High doses—lowered blood pressure and pulse rate, decreased breathing rate, nausea, vomiting, blurred vision, flicking up and down of the eyes, loss of balance, dizziness, violence, suicidal thoughts, seizures, coma, and death.

Long-term effects: Weight loss, mental health.

Other health issues: PCP has been linked to self-injury; risk of HIV, hepatitis, and other infectious diseases from shared needles.

Mental health issues: Memory loss (short term and long term), problems with speech and thinking, anxiety, depression.

In combination with alcohol: Increased risk of coma.

Withdrawal symptom: Headaches, sweating.

# Prescription Opioids

Commonly known as pain relievers, with an origin similar to that of heroin. Opioids can cause euphoria and are often used nonmedically, leading to overdose deaths. Street names—numerous. Commercial uses—codeine, fentanyl (Actiq, Duragesic, Sublimaze), hydrocodone or dihydrocodeinone (Vicodin, Lortab, Lorcet, and others), hydromorphone (Dilaudid), meperidine (Demerol), methadone (Dolophine, Methadose), morphine (Duramorph, Roxanol), oxycodone (OxyContin, Percodan, Percocet, and others), oxymorphne (Opana).

Short-term effects: Pain relief, drowsiness, constipation, euphoria, slowed breathing, death.

Long-term effects: Psychological or physical addiction, difficult withdrawal symptoms.

*Danger: Overdose may cause permanent brain damage, a coma, or death.*

Other health issues: Pregnant women—miscarriage, low birth weight, neonatal abstinence syndrome. Older adults—higher risk of accidental misuse or abuse because many older adults have multiple prescriptions, increasing the risk of drug-drug interactions, and breakdown of drugs slows with age. Many older adults are treated with prescription medications for pain. Risk of HIV, hepatitis, and other infectious diseases from shared needles.

Mental health issues: Confusion, paranoia, anxiety.

In combination with alcohol: Dangerous slowing of heart rate and breathing, leading to a coma or death.

Withdrawal symptom: Restlessness, muscle and bone pain, insomnia, diarrhea, vomiting, cold flashes with goose bumps ("cold turkey"), leg movements.

## Prescription Stimulants

Medications that increase alertness, attention, energy, blood pressure, heart rate, and breathing rate. Street names—bennies, black beauties, crosses, hearts, speed, uppers, skippy, vitamin R. Commercial uses—amphetamine (Adderall, Benzedrine), methylphenidate (Concerta, Ritalin).

Short-term effects: Increased alertness, attention, and energy, increased blood pressure and heart rate, narrowed blood vessels, increased blood sugar, opened-up breathing passages. High doses—dangerously high body temperature and irregular heartbeat, heart failure, and seizures.

Long-term effects: Heart problems, mental health issues.

Other health issues: Risk of HIV, hepatitis, and other infectious diseases from shared needles.

Mental health issues: Depression, anxiety, paranoia, anger, psychosis.

In combination with alcohol: Masks the depressant action of alcohol, increasing of alcohol overdose; may increase blood pressure and jitters.

Withdrawal symptom: Depression, tiredness, sleep problems.

## Psilocybin

A hallucinogen in certain types of mushrooms that grow in parts of South America, Mexico, and the United States. Street names—magic mushrooms, purple passion, shrooms. Commercial uses—none known.

Short-term effects: Muscle relaxation or weakness, problems with movement, enlarged pupils, nausea, vomiting, drowsiness.

68

Other health issues: Risk of poisoning if a poisonous mushroom is accidentally ingested.

Mental health issues: Hallucinations, paranoia, inability to tell fantasy from reality, panic attacks, altered perception of time.

In combination with alcohol: May decrease the perceived effects of alcohol.

Withdrawal symptom: Unknown.

# Rohypnol (Flunitrazepam)

A benzodiazepine chemically similar to prescription sedatives such as Valium and Xanax. Teens and young adults tend to use this drug at bars, nightclubs, concerts, and parties. It has been used to commit sexual assaults due to its ability to sedate and incapacitate unsuspecting victims. Street names—date rape drug, forget-me pill, La Rocha, Mexican Valium, mind eraser, R2, Reynolds, roaches, roofies, wolfies. Commercial uses—flunitrazepam (Rohypnol).

Short-term effects: Drowsiness, sedation, sleep, muscle relaxation, impaired reaction time and motor coordination, excitability, slurred speech, headache, slowed breathing and heart rate.

Long-term effects: Unknown.

*Danger: Overdose may cause permanent brain damage, a coma, or death.*

Other health issues: Unknown.

Mental health issues: Amnesia, anxiety, impaired mental functioning and judgment, confusion, aggression, tension, irritability, hallucinations, delirium.

In combination with alcohol: Severe sedation, unconsciousness, slowed heart rate and breathing, which can lead to death.

Withdrawal symptom: Headache, muscle pain, extreme anxiety, tension, restlessness, confusion, irritability, numbness and tingling of hands and feet, hallucinations, delirium, convulsions, seizures or shock.

## Salvia (*Salvia divinorum*)

A dissociative drug that is an herb in the mint family native to southern Mexico. Dissociative drugs are hallucinogens that cause the user to feel detached from reality. Street names—magic mint, Sally-D, shepherdess's herb, diviner's sage. Commercial uses—sold legally in most states as *Salvia divinorum*.

Short-term effects: Altered visual perception, body sensations, sweating.

Long-term effects: Unknown

Other health issues: Unknown

Mental health issues: Short-lived but intense hallucinations, mood swings, feelings of detachment from one's body.

In combination with alcohol: Unknown.

Withdrawal symptom: Unknown.

## Steroids (Anabolic)

Man-made substances used to treat conditions caused by low levels of steroid hormones in the body, and abused to enhance athletic and sexual performance and physical appearance. Street names—juice, pumpers, roids. Commercial uses—nandrolone (Oxandrin), oxandrolone (Anadrol), oxymetholone (Winstrol), stanozoloi (Durabolin), testosterone cypionate (Depo-Testosterone).

Short-term effects: Headache, acne, fluid retention (especially in the hands and feet), oily skin, yellowing of the skin and whites of the eyes, infection at the injection site.

Long-term effects: Kidney damage or failure, liver damage, high blood pressure, enlarged heart, or changes in cholesterol, leading to increased risk of stroke or heart attack.

Other health issues: Males—shrunken testicles, lowered sperm count, infertility, baldness, development of breasts, impaired judgment. Females—facial hair, male-pattern baldness, menstrual cycle changes, enlargement of the clitoris, deepened voice. Adolescents—stunted growth.

Mental health issues: Extreme mood swings, aggression, "roid rage," paranoia, jealousy, extreme irritability, delusions, impaired judgment, depression that may lead to suicide attempts.

In combination with alcohol: Increased risk of violent behavior.

Withdrawal symptom: Mood swings, tiredness, restlessness, loss of appetite, insomnia, lowered sex drive.

## Synthetic Cannabinoids

A wide variety of herbal mixtures containing man-made cannabinoid chemicals related to THC in marijuana, but often much stronger and more dangerous. Sometimes misleadingly called "synthetic marijuana" and marketed as a "natural," "safe," legal alternative to marijuana. Street names—K2, spice, black mamba, bliss, fake weed, fire, genie, moon rocks, Yucatan, Zohai. Commercial uses—none known.

Short-term effects: Increased heart rate, vomiting, increased blood pressure and reduced blood supply to the heart, heart attack.

Long-term effects: Unknown.

Other health issues: Use of synthetic cannabinoids has led to an increase in emergency room visits in certain areas.

Mental health issues: Depression, anxiety, agitation, confusion, hallucinations, anxiety, paranoia.

In combination with alcohol: Unknown.

Withdrawal symptom: Headaches, anxiety, depression, irritability.

## Synthetic Cathinones (Bath Salts)

An emerging family of drugs containing one or more synthetic chemicals related to cathinone, a stimulant found natural in the khat plant. Examples of such chemicals include mephedrone, methylone, and 3,4-methylenedioxypyrovalerone (MDPV). Street names—bloom, cloud nine, cosmic blast, flakka, vanilla sky, white lightning. Commercial uses—none known.

Short-term effects: Increased heart rate and blood pressure, euphoria, increased sociability and sex drive, sweating, nausea, vomiting, insomnia, irritability, dizziness, reduced motor control.

Long-term effects: Breakdown of skeletal muscle tissue, kidney failure, death.

Other health issues: Risk of HIV, hepatitis, and other infectious diseases from shared needles.

Mental health issues: Depression, anxiety, paranoia, hallucinations, agitation, psychotic and violent behavior, suicidal thoughts, panic attacks, clouded thinking.

In combination with alcohol: Unknown.

Withdrawal symptom: Depression, anxiety, problems sleeping, tremors, paranoia.

## Tobacco

Plant grown for its leaves, which are dried and fermented before use. Street names—none. Commercial uses—numerous brand names.

Short-term effects: Increased blood pressure, breathing, and heart rate.

Long-term effects: Greatly increases risk of cancer (lung cancer when smoked and oral cancers when chewed), chronic bronchitis, emphysema, heart disease, leukemia, cataracts, pneumonia.

Other health issues: Pregnant women—miscarriage, low birth weight, premature delivery, stillbirth, learning and behavior problems.

# How Am I Doing?

Please answer each question honestly and with as much detail as possible. Remember, the questions are designed to help you understand your lifestyle as it relates to your health and well-being. If the question does not pertain to your lifestyle, please explain what a negative impact drugs would have on your life if you did use them.

In the past, my drug use has negatively impacted my . . .

Health

_____

_____

_____

Finances

_____

_____

_____

Social relationships

_____

_____

_____

Professional paths

_____

_____

_____

It is important to closely monitor my consumption of alcohol, because . . .

_____

_____

_____

# A Call to Action!

Now, the real work begins! This is, in essence, your commitment to making a number of positive changes in your lifestyle.

I will make the following positive changes to improve my physical health:

1. _____ Beginning: _____

2. _____ Beginning: _____

3. _____ Beginning: _____

I will make the following positive changes to improve my mental and emotional health:

1. _____ Beginning: _____

2. _____ Beginning: _____

3. _____ Beginning: _____

I will make the following positive changes to improve my interpersonal relationships:

1. _____ Beginning: _____

2. _____ Beginning: _____

I will make the following positive changes to improve my career opportunities:

1. _____ Beginning: _____

2. _____ Beginning: _____

I will make the following positive changes to improve my self-image:

1. _____ Beginning: _____

2. _____ Beginning: _____

3. _____

Beginning: _____

# Section 4:
# Developing Effective Communication Skills

# DEVELOPING EFFECTIVE COMMUNICATION SKILLS

Possessing and practicing effective communication skills is a skill that enhances an individual's self-image. It helps to improve our significant relationships, provides us with the ability to function in social situations, and ensures that we achieve success in our professional lives. Effective communicators are known to experience less anxiety in all aspects of their lives and acquire personal and professional success as they possess the ability to openly express themselves in nonthreatening ways that serve to build strong connections with others. We all have the potential to further our capabilities in the workplace and cultivate stronger bonds with others through the art of effective communication. In this section, you will learn why certain communication styles are more successful than others and how finely honed communication skills can have a positive effect in all areas of our lives.

# Objectives

At the end of this section, the participant will be able to
1.  verbalize a clear understanding of the open systems communications model,
2.  identify the blocks and barriers to effective communications,
3.  identify the key elements of effective communications,
4.  identify ways you can improve your interpersonal communications, and
5.  demonstrate, in a classroom setting, effective interpersonal communication skills.

# INTERPERSONAL COMMUNICATION OPEN SYSTEMS MODEL

Responsibility for effective communication: _____ % sender, _____ % receiver

Sender _____ (message) _____ Receiver

Effective communication promotes a sense of trust at its core. We express ourselves in verbal and nonverbal ways throughout our lives, yet few of us have taken a formal course in this art form. Within this section, we will address the importance of communicating with others in a clear and concise manner, and the negative repercussions when we miscommunicate (or, perhaps missed communication).

Workplace Collapse

No matter what career field we are in, we must communicate with our coworkers, supervisors, and subordinates in a clear and concise manner. Ineffective communication creates confusion, tension, disruption, strained relationships, low productivity, and a hostile environment. Ultimately, it may result in the organization failing to meet its stated mission, which, in turn, causes people to lose their livelihoods.

Family Strains

Effective communication is the glue that holds relationships and families together. Regardless of what the cause, unaddressed miscommunication leads to confusion, dissatisfaction, helplessness, and hopelessness. Miscommunication is the number one reason that couples seek out and engage in therapy. It is a common factor in separations, incidents of domestic violence, infidelity, and divorce. We're not saying that there can never be instances when a message is incorrectly translated. That would be absurd! What we are saying is that both parties are responsible for openly and honestly communicating their thoughts and feelings, using effective listening skills, understanding and accepting one another's point of view, showing empathy, and being willing to compromise. These are all tenets of effective communication.

Children who are raised in an environment where there is poor communication, especially when one or both parents treat one another in a disrespectful and hostile manner become frightened, uncertain, and helpless. If the situation exists for a protracted period of time, they learn to compensate by using tobacco products, using illicit substances, abusing prescription medication, abusing alcohol, or experimenting sexually. Conversely, children who observe and are taught to utilize effective communication skills tend to do well in school, do not succumb to alcohol or drugs, do not use tobacco products, and possess a healthy self-image. In this section, we are going to look at barriers to effective communication and effective ways to improve your communication skills.

# COMMUNICATION INTERFERENCE

When one person sends a message to another person, the message must go through a series of filters, and may also be blocked by language and other barriers. Filters and barriers interfere with the message as it is transmitted by the sender along the pathway to the receiver. Let's take a closer look at what this really means.

First, we will address communication filters. Consider an air-conditioning filter. Its purpose is to screen out harmful chemicals and block them from polluting the air. Similarly, all the words we speak (including e-mails and text messages, etc.) pass through human filters, which means that not all the words reach the intended recipient. These filters are called biases, which are defined as "prejudice in favor of or against one thing, person, or group compared with another, usually in a way considered to be unfair." These prejudices include, but certainly are not limited to, our personal and professional values, distrust of certain individuals or groups, religious belief systems, feelings of superiority or inferiority, negative attitudes toward someone or something, positive attitudes toward someone or something, political leanings, racist/sexist/ageist beliefs, the other person's appearance, how a person is dressed, and a myriad of other beliefs. Biases interfere with effective communication in that they block us from fully listening to the other person. We tend to form judgments. We may discount them as individuals and consider what they have to say as irrelevant.

Every human being has at least some biases. List five of your strongest biases. Where did they come from? How are they interfering with your ability to communicate in an effective way?

| Biases | Origins | Negative consequences |
|---|---|---|
| _____ | _____ | _____ |
| _____ | _____ | _____ |
| _____ | _____ | _____ |
| _____ | _____ | _____ |
| _____ | _____ | _____ |

Let's carry this exercise a step further. Identify at least five biases that have served to discount, demean, or discredit you.

| Biases | How they affected you |
| --- | --- |
| _____ | _____ |
| _____ | _____ |
| _____ | _____ |
| _____ | _____ |

Next, we will address language barriers. These include, but are not limited to, foreign languages, sarcasm, humor, accents and regional dialects, slang, jargon, improper use of grammar, and using words incorrectly. Provide at least five examples of how language barriers have impaired your ability to communicate with another individual or group of individuals.

1. _____

2. _____

3. _____

4. _____

5. _____

Along with biases and language barriers, there are physical barriers to effective communication.

These may include noises (dog barking, baby crying, loud music, people yelling, etc.) and distance between you and the person with whom you are communicating (e.g., another room, e-mails, texts). Unmet physical needs can also be problematic (e.g., hungry, thirsty, tired, needing to use the restroom). Extreme cold and heat are physical barriers. Identify at least five occasions when physical barriers interfered with your ability to communicate effectively.

1. _____

2. _____

3. _____

4. _____

5. _____

A number of emotional and attitudinal factors may also be involved, including distress, feeling anxious, depressed or overwhelmed, mentally exhausted, inattentive, resistant to change, short on empathy, and conflicting emotional states. Another key factor is timing. The communication has to be about something current, and both parties have to be open to feedback at the same time.

Finally, there are cultural and ethnic barriers in play. Within every culture and ethnic group there are clearly defined expectations based on an individual's gender, status, and race, all of which dictate to whom you can and cannot communicate and in what manner. Gender most certainly has an impact on the way we converse with one another. Women tend to use the language of feelings, while men use the language of facts. Some cultures and ethnic groups prohibit women from speaking with a male not of their group. In most cultures throughout the world, persons from the lower classes are blocked from approaching and speaking with persons from the upper classes. Deferential treatment is accorded to those with social status (e.g., physicians, dentists, college professors, the elderly, elected officials, religious leaders, military personnel). There still exist areas of this country where one culture or race refuses to socialize with another. There can be dire consequences when someone, either intentionally or unintentionally, violates cultural and ethnic norms.

# POSITIVE BENEFITS OF COMMUNICATING EFFECTIVELY

We all benefit from communicating with another person or a group of people in a manner that ensures that the sender and receiver understand the message that is being sent. These benefits include the following:

- Reduction in level of frustration
- Increase in level of trust
- Less frequent misunderstandings
- Achievement of mutual understanding
- Positive and stronger relationships
- Increased levels of productivity
- Balanced mental and emotional states
- Enjoyment of mutual respect
- Reduction of anxiety levels
- Attainment of a higher level of consciousness
- An increase in mindfulness of the needs of others
- An increase in your social skills

Identify other benefits, to you and others. _____

_____

_____

_____

 The Harvard Business Review rated the ability to communicate the most important fact in making an employee promotable. They ranked it more important than ambition, education, and hard work.

# COMMUNICATION STYLE EXERCISE

It is important for you to be completely honest when selecting responses to each of the following scenarios. Select how you have responded or would respond to each situation, not a response that merely makes you look good!

Scenario 1. You order a meal in a restaurant, and the food is not cooked to your satisfaction. In this situation, I would usually

A) tell the server, in a polite manner, that a mistake was made, and ask the server to correct the order

B) be displeased, finish the meal, and say nothing to the server

C) make a snide or angry remark to the server, or perhaps bypass the server and ask to speak to the manager

Scenario 2. You are driving your vehicle when someone cuts you off. You pull up next to the individual who cut you off at the next stop light. In this situation, I would usually

A) roll down my window and yell at the driver or give him the finger

B) ignore the driver at the stoplight and feel relieved that the other vehicle didn't hit yours, and you soon forget that it happened

C) give dirty looks to the driver and stay in a state of anxiety for some time following the incident

Scenario 3. You are in a speed (ten-item) line at a grocery store. The person in front of you is slow in taking items out of her basket, waits until the items are rung up before presenting discount coupons, then writes a check for the amount. In this situation, I would usually

A) become irritated, make a smart comment, or perhaps set my basket down and walk out of the store

B) be curious about the other person's behavior but not let the experience affect my mood

C) become somewhat irritated or frustrated but don't show it or say anything to anyone

Scenario 4. You are engaged in a discussion with another person who has a very different opinion than you on a subject. In this situation, I would

A)  forcefully argue my point and not give in to the other person

B)  ask the person more about his or her viewpoint in a nonthreatening manner

C)  say nothing and probably make an excuse to leave


Scenario 5. You are at work and a supervisor tells you "you really screwed up" in front of your superiors, coworkers, or people who work under you. In this situation, I would

A)  feel embarrassed, frustrated, or angry but say nothing because I don't want to lose my job

B)  become angry and yell back at the person who made the comment

C)  remain calm and ask the individual to meet with you in private, to discuss the matter.


Scenario 6. You learn that a close friend—someone who is in a committed relationship with someone else—has been cheating on his or her partner. In this situation, I would

A)  say nothing—it's none of my business

B)  say nothing to the friend but tell his or her partner what you've heard

C)  tell the friend that you are disappointed in his or her behavior and that you don't know if you can remain friends

---

## Answers and Explanations

Remember that assertiveness is an important value to convey in difficult situations. All the above scenarios would be best handled using assertive communication skills instead of using aggressive or passive communication. Aggressiveness is a quality that can cause trouble for individuals and is not worth the stress it creates. Passiveness is a characteristic that prevents any positive change from occurring during demanding situations. For these reasons, assertiveness is what we must use in order to empower ourselves during tough circumstances. Which answers in each scenario are fueled by assertive behavior instead of aggressive or passive behavior?

Scenario 1

The answer showing assertiveness: A

The answer showing passiveness: B

The answer showing aggressiveness: C

Scenario 2

The answer showing assertiveness: B

The answer showing passiveness: C

The answer showing aggressiveness: A

Scenario 3

The answer showing assertiveness: B

The answer showing passiveness: C

The answer showing aggressiveness: A

Scenario 4

The answer showing assertiveness: B

The answer showing passiveness: C

The answer showing aggressiveness: A

Scenario 5

The answer showing assertiveness: C

The answer showing passiveness: A

The answer showing aggressiveness: B

Scenario 6

The answer showing assertiveness: C

The answer showing passiveness: A

The answer showing aggressiveness: B

Now go through the answers given above and determine what type of communication you are prone to use when dealing with difficult situations.

What kind of communicator are you? _____

# AGGRESSIVE COMMUNICATOR PROFILE

Aggressive communicators tend to do the following:
- Believe that their needs are paramount
- Constantly criticize or find fault with the people around them
- Use their positions of power to control other people
- Behave in mentally, emotionally, and sometimes physically abusive ways

What do aggressive communicators look like?
- Voice: loud, threatening, uses profanity excessively
- Attitude: hostile, demanding
- Physical stance: imposing, threatening, arms crossed
- Eye contact: glaring, staring down the other person
- Humor: used to ridicule or demean others

What are some of the advantages of being an aggressive communicator?
- They tend to get their own way, most of the time.
- Other people feel intimidated and give in to them.
- They control most conversations.

What are the disadvantages of being an aggressive communicator?
- Few people rally around when they are in need of support.
- They miss out experiencing deep intimacy in relationships.
- They are at a high risk for a heart condition, cancer, ulcers, etc.
- Others celebrate when they make a mistake.

What thoughts do aggressive communicators most often experience?
- "I'm important, you are not"; a sense of entitlement.

What feelings do aggressive communicators most often experience?
- Anger, resentment

What behaviors do aggressive communicators most often display?
- Manipulate others to get their own way

# PASSIVE COMMUNICATOR PROFILE

Passive communicators tend to do the following:
- Believe their rights are not as important as other people's
- Avoid conflict and confrontation
- Feel that they have no position of power
- Seldom have their own wants and needs met

Passive communicators tend to have poor self-esteem or a low self-image, feel at times as if they are invisible, and have unhealthy interpersonal relationships.

What does a passive communicator look like?
- Voice: soft, whispers, sometimes stutters
- Attitude: reserved, unassuming, introverted
- Physical stance: slumped shoulders
- Eye contact: looks down or away from others
- Humor: self-effacing

What are some of the advantages of being a passive communicator?
- Not taking risks is a safe way to go through life.
- Other people don't feel intimidated by them.
- It takes very little effort to be passive.

What are some of the disadvantages of being a passive communicator?
- Other people are unaware when they are in need of support.
- Other people make decisions for them.
- They are often predictable, thus can be easily manipulated.
- They experience difficulty coping with unplanned situations.

What thoughts do passive communicators most often experience?
- "I'm not important, everyone else is important."

What feelings do passive communicators often experience?
- Fear of the unknown; powerlessness; loneliness

What behaviors do passive communicators most often display?
- Let themselves be manipulated by other people

# ASSERTIVE COMMUNICATOR PROFILE

Assertive communicators tend to do the following:
- Protect their rights and the rights of others
- Be willing to compromise
- Share power with others
- Accept responsibility for their actions

What does an assertive communicator look like?
- Voice: modulated, nonthreatening
- Attitude: exudes self-confidence, optimist
- Physical stance: open
- Eye contact: obtains and maintains eye contact
- Humor: sensitive to the feelings of others

What are some of the advantages of being an assertive communicator?
- They use negotiation and conflict resolution skills.
- They enjoy healthy interpersonal relationships.
- They respect the thoughts and feelings of others.
- They are respected by others.

What are some of the disadvantages of being an assertive communicator?
- They may be "attacked" by people who are less self-assured.
- May be perceived as "unreal" by pessimists and unsuccessful people.
- Insecure people may feel threatened by their optimism and positive energy.
- Their calmness may be perceived as a weakness.

What thoughts do assertive communicators most often experience?
- "We are equally important."

What feelings do assertive communicators often experience?
- Optimistic outlook on life; contentment

What behaviors do assertive communicators most often display?
- Mutual respect

We listen to people at a rate of 125-250 words per minute, but think at 1,000-3,000 words per minute.

# ASSERTIVE COMMUNICATION PRACTICUM

It is time to practice using assertive communication techniques. Relax. Take a deep breath. Try not to hyperventilate. You will not be graded. When you are ready, your facilitator will assign you and another class member a role. (If you are not in a classroom setting, select someone to role play with you.) Before you begin, there are some guidelines that we ask you to follow: (1) take your assigned role seriously, (2) do not add anything to the script, (3) do not remove anything from the script, and (4) stay within your assigned role.

Script 1 situation: You make an easily corrected mistake at work.
Your supervisor: "You never do anything right!"
Your response: _____

Script 2 situation: You don't want to visit your partner's relatives.
Partner's response: "Why are you being so selfish?"
Your response: _____

Script 3 situation: You believe that you are worth more than you are being paid.
You to your supervisor: "I want a pay raise."
Your supervisor's response: _____

Script 4 situation: You have received poor service at a very nice restaurant.
The server: "Is there anything else I can get you?"
Your feedback to the server: _____

Script 5 situation: You are merely "window shopping" at an appliance store.
The salesperson repeatedly tries to get you interested in buying something.
Your response: _____

We derive 55% of a message's meaning from the speaker's facial expressions, 38% from how the communicator says the message, and 7% from the actual words spoken. (This fact could be the reason behind miscommunication in text messages or phone calls.)

# Section 5:
# The Language of Feelings

# THE LANGUAGE OF FEELINGS

By understanding our own feelings, we can learn to let go of past suffering and move toward emotional wellness in the future. The art of understanding what we are feeling, as well as the ability to communicate this to others, is a talent that greatly enhances our emotional and mental well-being. In this section, you will identify your wide range of feelings and how they affect you and those around you and learn how to implement the language of feelings.

The language of feelings is a relatively new concept. It involves correctly identifying what you are feeling in any given situation, and communicating this to others in a clear and concise manner.

# Objectives

At the end of this section, the participant will be able to
1.  verbalize a clear understanding of the calm-to-anger continuum,
2.  identify feelings that occur along the continuum,
3.  identify the order in which the feelings occur along the continuum,
4.  identify what feelings you would experience in a variety of settings and identify how you might react differently in the future, and
5.  demonstrate, in a classroom setting, the ability to communicate your feelings to others, utilizing the language of feelings.

# Sources of Anger

+ Glutamate is abundant throughout the human body but particularly in the nervous system and the brain. It is the body's principal neurotransmitter. Glutamate is important for neural communication, memory formation, learning, and self-regulation. Glutamate deficiencies can cause a variety of neurological disorders including attention-deficit hyperactivity disorder (ADHD), seizures, multiple sclerosis, autism, diabetes, Parkinson disease, Huntington disease, and schizophrenia.

+ GABA (gamma-amino butyric acid) is an amino acid that helps keep us calm and relaxed. GABA deficiency may cause anxiety or panic attacks, which can also lead to outbursts of anger.

+ Acetylcholine is a neurotransmitter that can be found in the brain and the peripheral nervous system. It is involved in learning and memory; it also stimulates muscle tissue. (Acetylcholine is associated with Alzheimer's disease.) Low levels of this neurotransmitter can impede proper brain functioning and have been found in individuals with anger management issues. Ginseng and *Ginkgo biloba* are natural alternatives that can elevate levels of acetylcholine in the body and brain.

+ Serotonin is found mainly in the central nervous system and the gastrointestinal (GI) tract; it is used to help manage digestion, mood, sleep, appetite, learning, and memory.

+ Norepinephrine is produced by the adrenal gland and is responsible for transporting nerve impulses between neurons. It can be found in both the central and sympathetic nervous systems. Norepinephrine also behaves as a stress hormone, raising a person's heart rate and blood flow to the muscles. It stimulates the release of blood sugar (oftentimes it is compared to adrenaline).

+ Dopamine is produced by the brain and it plays a critical role in the functioning of the central nervous system. It is also linked with the intricate system of motivation and reward within the brain. Abnormal levels can cause ADHD and Parkinson disease, as well as other disorders.

 **FUN FACT** | The Pope tweets in 9 languages.

# Hormones

+ Testosterone may make us more aggressive, without us consciously feeling any aggression; it may make someone less tolerant.

+ Higher levels of estrogen are linked with increased aggression in women and men.

+ Low insulin (hypoglycemia) is associated with irritability, aggression, and confusion.

+ Cortisol is a stress hormone and helps curb reactions to life stressors.

# Genetic

+ Childhood abuse (physical, emotional, mental, or sexual) may contribute to the development of a "warrior gene."

# Brain Damage

+ Deep brain injury

+ Lesions in frontal and temporal lobes

+ Diffuse/minimal brain dysfunction

+ Trauma (emotional or physical)

# Environmental (Family and Cultural Training)

+ Angry modeling within the family may produce habituation and desensitization.

+ Anger is an acceptable emotion for males but not females.

+ A person is raised in a "volatile" culture or subculture.

+ A person is raised in a "survival" subculture.

+ Anger begets anger later in life.

The following is a list of common feelings that most of us experience between the states of calm and anger, along with their definitions. It is generally believed that we experience seven to ten feelings when transitioning these states and that they occur on both a conscious and a subconscious level.

| | |
|---|---|
| Abused | being spoken to in an insulting or offensive manner |
| Affronted | being offended by an intentional act or word |
| Afraid | filled with fear or apprehension |
| Agitated | feeling troubled; highly upset at a person or a situation |
| Aggrieved | caused to be sorrowful |
| Aggravated | greatly annoyed or irritated |
| Ambivalent | conflicting feelings toward a person or thing (e.g., love and hate) |
| Angry | extreme displeasure resulting from injury, mistreatment opposition, etc., creating a desire to fight back |
| Anguished | experiencing/expressing severe mental/physical pain or suffering |
| Anxious | uneasy, apprehensive, or worried about what may happen |
| Ashamed | feeling shame, sheepish |
| Astonished | greatly surprised or impressed |
| Awkward | feeling out of place, clumsy |
| Chagrined | a feeling of vexation, marked by disappointment or humiliation |
| Confused | mixed up mentally; disordered thoughts |
| Defenseless | without defense or protection; totally vulnerable |
| Defensive | self-justifying; oversensitive |
| Dejected | sad and depressed; dispirited |
| Depressed | low spirits; gloominess; dejection; ongoing sadness |
| Discontent | restless desire for something more or different; uneasy in mind |
| Disgraced | condition of feeling out of favor; state of being dishonored |

| | |
|---|---|
| Disgusted | feeling a strong distaste; aversion or repugnance produced by something loathsome |
| Disillusioned | disappointed in someone or something that one discovers to be less than good than one had believed it would be |
| Disregarded | thoughts or feelings are paid no attention; ignored |
| Disrespected | being treated in a discourteous or insolent manner |
| Distraught | extremely troubled; mentally confused |
| Distressed | suffering from emotional or mental discomfort |
| Embarrassed | self-conscious, confused, and ill at ease |
| Endangered | in the midst of a perceived dangerous situation |
| Envious | discontent because of another's advantages, possessions, etc. |
| Exasperated | intense frustration or irritation |
| Fearful | anxiety caused by the presence/nearness of danger, evil, pain, etc. |
| Frightened | startled; alarmed |
| Frustrated | prevented from gratifying certain impulses or desires |
| Furious | full of anger |
| Guilty | the state of having done a wrong or committed an offense |
| Helpless | not able to help oneself; lacking help or protection |
| Hopeless | feeling or causing despair about something |
| Humiliated | feeling of being treated in an indignant way |
| Hurt | injured mentally; something painful or that causes suffering |
| Ignored | disregarded intentionally; refused to be noticed |
| Inadequate | unable to deal with a given situation |
| Indignant | reaction to being wronged; reaction to an injustice |
| Inept | feeling incompetent; lacking in ability |
| Inferior | feeling lower than another, in status or in position |

| | |
|---|---|
| Infuriated | extremely angry |
| Insulted | spoken to or treated with disrespect or scornful abuse |
| Intimidated | frightened or overawed by someone else, especially when being pressured into doing what someone else wants |
| Irritated | extremely annoyed or exasperated |
| Jealous | resentfully suspicious of a rival or a rival's influence |
| Lonely | feeling emotionally apart from others; isolated |
| Mad | expressing a strong negative emotion |
| Mortified | caused to feel extremely embarrassed or humiliated |
| Outraged | feeling injured or wronged; gross violation of decency |
| Overwhelmed | a deep feeling of being overcome, crushed, overpowered |
| Overwrought | exhausted by intense emotions |
| Panicked | a sudden, overwhelming fear, with or without cause |
| Perplexed | completely baffled; very puzzled |
| Powerless | lack of power over someone or something |
| Rejected | one's thoughts or feelings are being dismissed |
| Resentful | indignant displeasure toward a person or an event |
| Restless | characterized by inability to rest or relax; uneasy; unquiet |
| Ridiculed | spoken to in a demeaning manner; being made fun of |
| Sad | having, expressing, or showing low spirits or sorrow |
| Shocked | caused to feel surprised and upset |
| Skeptical | habitually doubting; not easily persuaded or convinced |
| Slighted | one's thoughts or feelings are treated as trivial or unimportant |
| Stupid | thinking of oneself as slow-witted, dull, foolish, or irrational |
| Threatened | to have a threat uttered against someone |
| Trepidation | a feeling of fear or agitation about something that may happen |

| | |
|---|---|
| Uncertain | not sure or certain in knowledge; self-doubting |
| Vulnerable | susceptible to physical or emotional attack or harm |
| Worried | to feel uneasy or concerned about something; to be troubled |
| Worthless | feeling undeserving of something, or undervalued by others |

# Is It Anger?

Step 1. Describe, in detail, the last time that you became angry.

_____

_____

_____

_____

_____

_____

_____

_____

_____

_____

_____

_____

_____

_____

_____

_____

_____

_____

Step 2. Referring to the feelings list, identify those feelings that you experienced before you became angry and explain why you experienced this feeling.

Feeling          Explanation

_____        because _____

_____

_____        because _____

_____

_____        because _____

_____

_____        because _____

_____

_____        because _____

_____

_____        because _____

_____

_____        because _____

_____

_____        because _____

_____

Step 3. Now, the most difficult step in this process is identifying in what order you experienced these feelings. Once you've identified the order, place them along the calm-to-anger continuum, in chronological order.

Example:

1-confused    3-disappointed    5-annoyed    7-indignant

Calm _____Anger

2-frustrated    4-helpless    6-disregarded    8-resentful

Calm _____Anger

Step 4. The next four or five times you experience an episode of anger, wait until you are calm, then repeat steps one through three on separate sheets of paper.

Step 5. Place all the calm-to-anger continuum sheets side by side. This will help you identify patterns in your feelings. Additionally, you will identify your "triggers"—words other people use that elicit the same emotional responses from you. You might consider that other people may have already identified this pattern, and can use this knowledge to manipulate your emotions, if they so choose. Take a risk. Learn to be unpredictable!

Step 6. The final stage of the evolutionary process! Begin using the language of feelings—telling other people what you are feeling, in the moment. We have provided some phrases that work well for us.

Caution: In the language of feelings, it is very important that you begin each statement with the personal pronoun "I" instead of "you."

"I am confused why you continually ask me to close up the restaurant when everyone else gets to leave at eleven o'clock."

"I felt hurt when you called me stupid."

"I feel very alone when you go days without speaking to me."

"I feel disregarded when you ask for my opinion then ignore what I say."

"I feel frightened and insecure when you visit your ex-spouse."

# What Am I Feeling and Why?
Please be completely honest when responding to each scenario.

Scenario 1. Your friend asks to borrow your vehicle for the night. You loan him the vehicle, under the condition that he return it no later than 9:00 a.m. because you have errands to run before leaving for work. By 2:00 p.m. the friend has not returned the vehicle, and he isn't answering your phone calls or text messages, yet he knows that you have to be at work by 4:00 p.m. At 3:30 p.m. you begin walking to work and end up being very late. Your boss yells at you and won't accept any excuses. You return home from work at 11:00 p.m., and find your vehicle parked in front of your house/apartment.

What feelings are you experiencing? _____

_____

How would you handle this situation? _____

_____

Identify at least two repercussions of handling this situation in this way.

_____     _____

What would be a more effective way to handle this situation if it occurred in the future?

_____

_____

Scenario 2. You had a stressful day at work and can't wait to get home and relax. On the way home, you are stopped for speeding and given a ticket. The officer was quite rude to you, on the verge of being a bully.

What feelings are you experiencing? _____

_____

How would you handle this situation? _____

_____

Identify at least two repercussions of handling this situation in this way.

_____          _____

What would be a more effective way to handle this situation if it occurred in the future?

_____

_____

Scenario 3. Your supervisor calls you into her office and starts yelling at you for a mistake she assumes that you made, but you know that it was made by another employee.

What feelings are you experiencing? _____

_____

How would you handle this situation? _____

_____

Identify at least two repercussions of handling this situation in this way.

_____          _____

What would be a more effective way to handle this situation if it occurred in the future?

_____

_____

Ancient doctors believed that different organs controlled certain moods. Happiness, for example, came from the heart, anger from the liver, and fear from the kidneys.

Scenario 4. You have been waiting in a checkout line at your favorite store for about ten minutes. Someone cuts in front of you, and the cashier serves that person. Neither the customer nor the cashier offered an explanation for this behavior.

What feelings are you experiencing? _____

_____

How would you handle this situation? _____

_____

Identify at least two repercussions of handling this situation in this way.

_____        _____

What would be a more effective way to handle this situation if it occurred in the future?

_____

_____

Scenario 5. You call your mom to see how she's doing. Throughout the conversation, she complains about life, that no one cares about her, and "you never call or visit."

What feelings are you experiencing? _____

_____

How would you handle this situation? _____

_____

Identify at least two repercussions of handling this situation in this way.

_____        _____

**FUN FACT** Studies show that if people adjust their facial expression to reflect an emotion, they actually begin to feel that emotion.

What would be a more effective way to handle this situation if it occurred in the future?

_____

_____

Scenario 6. You are at a sporting event, watching your favorite team play. A fan sitting behind you is cheering for the opposing team, heckles your favorite player, and will not stop.

What feelings are you experiencing? _____

_____

How would you handle this situation? _____

_____

Identify at least two repercussions of handling this situation in this way.

_____     _____

What would be a more effective way to handle this situation if it occurred in the future?

_____

_____

Scenario 7. You worked very hard on a work project. You are very proud of what you accomplished and excited to show your finished product to your supervisor. However, on your day off a coworker takes the product to your supervisor and claims it as his own work. To top it off, he receives a promotion!

What feelings are you experiencing? _____

_____

How would you handle this situation? _____

_____

Identify at least two repercussions of handling this situation in this way.

_____     _____

What would be a more effective way to handle this situation if it occurred in the future?

_____

_____

Scenario 8. You are at a party and your partner is flirting with your friend.

What feelings are you experiencing? _____

_____

How would you handle this situation? _____

_____

Identify at least two repercussions of handling this situation in this way.

_____     _____

What would be a more effective way to handle this situation if it occurred in the future?

_____

_____

Scenario 9. Three teenagers have been taking a shortcut to a local park, through your manicured front lawn. This behavior has been going on every day for the past few weeks, even after you politely asked them to stop using your lawn as a shortcut.

What feelings are you experiencing? _____

_____

How would you handle this situation? _____

_____

Identify at least two repercussions of handling this situation in this way.

_____     _____

What would be a more effective way to handle this situation if it occurred in the future?

_____

_____

Scenario 10. An aunt suddenly passed away without leaving a will or telling anyone how she wanted her personal belongings divvied up. You and your sibling are going through items at her house and discover that you both want one of her family heirlooms.

What feelings are you experiencing? _____

_____

How would you handle this situation? _____

_____

Identify at least two repercussions of handling this situation in this way.

_____     _____

 **FUN FACT** Emotions are contagious. Negative or unpleasant emotions are more contagious than neutral or positive emotions.

What would be a more effective way to handle this situation if it occurred in the future?

_____

_____

Scenario 11. You receive a call from the principal at your child's school, reporting that your child was caught cheating on an examination and is being suspended for one day.

What feelings are you experiencing? _____

_____

How would you handle this situation? _____

_____

Identify at least two repercussions of handling this situation in this way.

_____   _____

What would be a more effective way to handle this situation if it occurred in the future?

_____

_____

Scenario 12. You come upon a LGBTQ rally outside your grocery store. They are protesting because the grocery store refuses to hire an LGBTQ person. The protesters are blocking the entrance to the store, but you need to purchase groceries for tonight's dinner. Oh, it is also the only grocery store in town.

What feelings are you experiencing? _____

_____

How would you handle this situation? _____

_____

Identify at least two repercussions of handling this situation in this way.

_____     _____

What would be a more effective way to handle this situation if it occurred in the future?

_____

_____

**Scenario 13.** You and the person you are in a committed relationship with are planning on taking your first vacation together to visit your family. Your partner believes that you should pay for the entire trip, even though you both earn about the same amount of money.

What feelings are you experiencing? _____

_____

How would you handle this situation? _____

_____

Identify at least two repercussions of handling this situation in this way.

_____     _____

What would be a more effective way to handle this situation if it occurred in the future?

_____

_____

**Scenario 14.** You are driving on a public road, when someone cuts you off. You slam on your brakes and skid off the road. You are not hurt, and your vehicle is not damaged.

What feelings are you experiencing? _____

_____

How would you handle this situation? _____

_____

Identify at least two repercussions of handling this situation in this way.

_____     _____

What would be a more effective way to handle this situation if it occurred in the future?

_____

_____

Scenario 15. You and a friend go to a restaurant to eat. A server tells you she will be right with you. She disappears and you have to go find her. You place your order. When it arrives the food is not prepared the way that you ordered it.

What feelings are you experiencing? _____

_____

How would you handle this situation? _____

_____

Identify at least two repercussions of handling this situation in this way. _____

What would be a more effective way to handle this situation, if it occurred in the future?

_____

_____

In the English language, there are more than 400 words assigned to emotions and sentiments.

Scenario 16. You are in a movie theater. The movie starts. Suddenly the person sitting in front of you takes out a cell phone and begins playing a game. The light from the phone is distracting you.

What feelings are you experiencing? _____

_____

How would you handle this situation? _____

_____

Identify at least two repercussions of handling this situation in this way.

_____    _____

What would be a more effective way to handle this situation, if it occurred in the future?

_____

_____

Scenario 17. You are sitting in an upscale bar with your date and another couple—people your date has never met. Your date's behavior embarrasses you, and the other couple show their annoyance (raising their eyebrows, rolling their eyes, etc.).

What feelings are you experiencing? _____

_____

How would you handle this situation? _____

_____

Identify at least two repercussions of handling this situation in this way.

_____    _____

**FUN FACT** Your heart beats 101,000 times a day. During your lifetime, it will beat about 3 billion times and pump about 800 million pints of blood.

What would be a more effective way to handle this situation if it occurred in the future?

_____

_____

Scenario 18. A coworker brings up a political topic and asks you for your opinion. You give your honest opinion, and the coworker verbally attacks your point of view.

What feelings are you experiencing? _____

_____

How would you handle this situation? _____

_____

Identify at least two repercussions of handling this situation in this way.

_____     _____

What would be a more effective way to handle this situation if it occurred in the future?

_____

_____

Scenario 19. Your significant other received a plus-one invitation to her best friend's wedding. You agree to accompany her. A few days before the wedding, you realize that you were scheduled to conduct training at your company the same day. Your significant other is hurt and embarrassed that you will not be attending the wedding. She says, "What am I going to tell everyone? I don't want to go by myself. That will look odd."

What feelings are you experiencing? _____

_____

How would you handle this situation? _____

Identify at least two repercussions of handling this situation in this way.

_____     _____

What would be a more effective way to handle this situation if it occurred in the future?

_____

_____

**Scenario 20.** Your partner of a few months can't stand your best friend of many years, and tells you in no uncertain terms that the friend is not welcome in your home.

What feelings are you experiencing? _____

_____

How would you handle this situation? _____

_____

Identify at least two repercussions of handling this situation in this way.

_____     _____

What would be a more effective way to handle this situation if it occurred in the future?

_____

_____

# Section 6:
# Making Rational Decisions

# MAKING RATIONAL DECISIONS

Making decisions without thoroughly thinking through the consequences is a human frailty. Some impulsive actions, such as reacting to an unexpected and dangerous situation, are not what this section is addressing. These actions are borne of our genetically engineered fight-or-flight responses to peril. What we wish to address are those decisions we make that have negative consequences in one or more aspects of our lives (e.g., financial stability, physical health, mental well-being, etc.). We have all, at least one time in our lives, been pressured by a salesperson or someone else who wants us to make a decision before we have time to collect all the facts. Some of us have succumbed to the pressure and are now owners of an item that we neither wanted nor needed. These pressures will present themselves throughout all our lives. In this section, we will be addressing strategies that you can employ in order to resist impulses, especially those that have the potential for harm.

# Objectives

At the end of this section, the participant will be able to

1.  identify past situations in which we did not practice effective impulse control,
2.  identify past situations in which we practiced effective impulse control,
3.  understand the difference between wants and needs, and
4.  identify past situations when meeting a want failed to fulfill our needs.

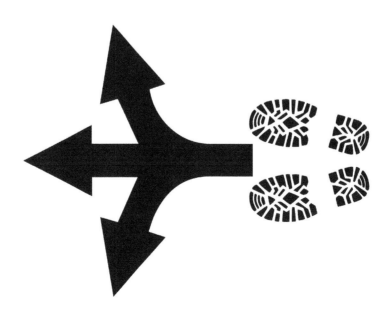

# *MAKING RATIONAL DECISIONS*

When we act impulsively in the face of difficult decisions or conflicts, we miss out on the opportunity to improve our lifestyles. Our lives are filled with important decisions. Acting impulsively on any of them makes for much more distress and complication than is necessary. For most people, impulsive decisions stem simply from getting caught up in what we want right now without thinking ahead, not thinking about the potential consequences of our actions.

How often have you had the reflective thought, "Well, it seemed like a good idea at the time"? Impulsive decisions affect our lives much more often than we think. Reckless sexual behavior or starting an affair with a coworker, hanging out with the wrong crowd or choosing to get drunk before an important meeting, spending this month's salary on something unnecessary or falling into debt as a result of overspending, eating unhealthy foods or disregarding exercise, procrastinating an important project or ignoring health concerns—all these actions are impulsive decisions that may have long-term, harmful consequences in our lives. We can all agree that life is less stressful when it is not filled with regret about our past decisions.

To avoid harm and regret, we must be proactive when making important decisions in our lives. It is the first step on the path toward living a happier and more productive life. Making rational decisions instead of impulsive ones starts with knowing who we are as individuals. Having a good sense of self can give us a clear idea of how much work we need to invest in changing impulsive habits. Some people are more impulsive than others, and some are more impulsive in certain situations than others.

Identify those areas of your life where impulsivity was a real concern. Ask yourself, "Am I most impulsive when attending parties, at my place of work, at home, or in a bar?" Then consider who is around you when you are making these decisions. Is it a particular friend, a group of individuals, or when you are alone?

I am most impulsive when I am . . .

_____

_____

_____

I make the most impulsive decisions when I am with . . .

_____

_____

_____

Additionally, it is important to identify those times when you find yourself being most rational. It is this rationality that we want to establish in all aspects of our lives. Map out the areas where rationality tends to drive your decision-making. Determine why you might be rational in one aspect of your life and impulsive in another.

I am less impulsive when I am . . .

_____

_____

_____

I make less impulsive decisions when I am with . . .

_____

_____

_____

Why do you think you are rational in some aspects of your life and impulsive in others? What is the difference between these instances where you choose rationality and the instances where you act impulsively?

_____

_____

_____

_____

_____

_____

Take a closer look at past impulsive decisions. Please describe the last three incidents in which your own impulsive decisions negatively impacted your life.

## Incident 1

_____

_____

_____

How did this incident impact your life?

_____

_____

_____

## Incident 2

_____

_____

_____

How did this incident impact your life?

_____

_____

_____

In 1567, the man said to have the longest beard in the world died after he tripped over his beard running away from a fire. (Think before you act!

## Incident 3

_____

_____

_____

How did this incident impact your life?

_____

_____

_____

Impulsive decisions can really have an impact on our lives, even if we do not realize it at the moment we make the decision. That is why we must actively work toward using rationality instead of impulsivity when making decisions. But how do we recognize our own impulsivity before we make those poor decisions?

One way to recognize this behavior is through understanding the distinction between wants and needs. According to the _Merriam-Webster Dictionary_, a "want" is defined as having a strong desire for something. A "need" is a lack of means of subsistence. In every aspect of life, the two concepts are opposing elements. Oftentimes, people have heard about this distinction when learning about financial responsibility—do I need this big screen television or is it just something that I want to spend my money on? Yet the contrast between wants and needs can apply to all aspects of our lives, even when it does not relate to material things. While impulse buying is a common toxic behavior in our society, it is not the only impulsive behavior that is a result of putting our wants above our needs.

Both our wants and needs are fueled by the amount of money we have. The contrast between them becomes jumbled when we see our money as our abilities to obtain these things. With the acquisition of more money, our wants start to become our needs, and oftentimes our needs then become less significant. In a society powered by money, it becomes difficult to avoid the convention of purchasing all our wants. It is important to step back and evaluate all we have so that we can distance ourselves from our consumerist culture.

## Needs

The obvious necessities that every person needs to stay alive—food, water, air, protection from the elements, good health—and not much else. When we fail to meet these needs, we fail to survive. However, we each have our own circumstances that dictate some other needs. Some individuals need reliable transportation to and from work. Others need constant medical care for chronic illnesses or pains. Most people have to follow a certain dress code, if they want to retain their jobs. Some people may list physical exercise as a priority because it helps them maintain a healthy lifestyle. It is also important to remember that we need happiness and mental acuity to maintain balance in our lives. Our emotional well-being is something that we can achieve through a clear understanding of our values, attitudes, and behaviors. Many of these "needs" are not considered basic, but they are things that we need in order to be responsible and healthy adults. It requires a certain level of maturity to determine what these needs are, but this develops over time and as we put in the effort.

For your particular job, health concerns, and family situation, what do you *need*?

1. _____
2. _____
3. _____
4. _____
5. _____
6. _____
7. _____
8. _____

## Wants

Everything else is a want. Now, there are levels of wants. Some of your wants might be nearer to needs than others. For instance, I want a new computer. Many people might say that they need a new computer to do homework or complete work-related tasks, but that's not true. Your computer may be old and not as fast and sleek as the newest models, but it remains functional. Even if the computer is completely dead, there are other computers that are available to the general public that you can use with relative ease. It is often the acquisition of something "new and improved" that compels us to buy, buy, buy! Another instance of a want that is oftentimes translated into a need is alcoholic beverages. Oftentimes, individuals use alcohol to cope with difficult circumstances or troubles. When someone says, "I need a drink," he or she really means, "I want a drink."

Life's stressors can be better resolved through exercise, eating healthy foods, or engaging in a deep conversation with a close friend.

Wants can relate to any behavior or attitude, toxic or otherwise, held by an individual. They are not necessarily bad, but they can be harmful when meeting a want detracts from meeting a need. When coupled with poor impulse control, these wants can become dangerous and harmful to our well-being. An individual with a want of sex makes an impulsive decision that he or she wants it right that moment, and commits an act of sexual assault. An individual with a want of power makes an impulsive decision that he or she wants that power over his or her partner and commits an act of domestic violence. An individual with a want of drugs makes an impulsive decision to buy illegal substances from a known drug dealer and gets arrested.

All impulsive decisions have their consequences. Thus, it is imperative to know your own wants so that you are aware of their possible harmful effects, should you make an impulsive decision to satisfy those wants.

What are your greatest *wants*?

1. _____

2. _____

3. _____

4. _____

5. _____

"Great things are not done by impulse, but by a series of small things brought together." – Vincent Van Gogh

# WANTS VS. NEEDS

Now we will practice choosing between wants and needs. For each item given below, decide if it is a want or a need. Then think about if you have ever considered the wants in this exercise needs.

1.   Food                    WANT? _____    NEED? _____

2.   Satellite dish          WANT? _____    NEED? _____

3.   Childcare               WANT? _____    NEED? _____

4.   House payment/rent      WANT? _____    NEED? _____

5.   Marijuana               WANT? _____    NEED? _____

6.   Washer/dryer            WANT? _____    NEED? _____

7.   Boat                    WANT? _____    NEED? _____

8.   Running water           WANT? _____    NEED? _____

9.   Video games             WANT? _____    NEED? _____

10.  Cell phone              WANT? _____    NEED? _____

11.  Health                  WANT? _____    NEED? _____

12.  Sound system in car     WANT? _____    NEED? _____

13.  Vacation                WANT? _____    NEED? _____

14.  Power                   WANT? _____    NEED? _____

"To change any behavior we have to slow down and act intentionally rather than from habit and impulse."

# Wants vs. Needs: Answer Sheet

| | |
|---|---|
| 1. Need | 8. Need |
| 2. Want | 9. Want |
| 3. Need | 10. Want |
| 4. Need | 11. Need |
| 5. Want | 12. Want |
| 6. Want | 13. Want |
| 7. Want | 14. Want |

# DECISION-MAKING SCENARIOS

Now that you understand the situations in which you are most impulsive and the difference between wants vs. needs, let's test your rational decision-making abilities. Below, there are three scenarios in which a difficult decision must be reached. How will you avoid impulsivity and come to a rational decision?

1.  Charlie has a final exam on Monday that encompasses more than eight hundred pages of material and 10 chapters. His boss scheduled him to work Saturday morning and Sunday afternoon, and he refuses to let him take the weekend off to study. Charlie is nervous about his grade in the class, and he has had very few hours of study time thus far. If he does not do well on this exam, Charlie will fail out of medical school. To make the problem worse, there is a huge party on Saturday that Charlie really wants to attend.

Based on the scenario, identify the problem that would require a decision:

_____

_____

Identify three solutions to Charlie's problem:

Solution A: _____

Solution B: _____

Solution C: _____

Of the solutions you have identified, which gives Jean the best outcome, and why?

_____

_____

2.  Anne's mother is sick in the hospital, back in her hometown in Massachusetts. Anne now lives in Florida. She is very worried about her mother and needs to visit her. She found out that the plane tickets are $400, and she had been saving her money for the

past few months so that she could get ahead on her apartment rent. Anne's landlord had already told her that, if she is late with her rent again, he will evict her. If she takes off more than a few days, her boss will not consider her for a promotion that she has been in line for.

Based on the scenario, identify the problem that would require a decision:

_____

_____

Identify three solutions to Anne's problem:

Solution A: _____

Solution B: _____

Solution C: _____

Of the solutions you have identified, which gives Jean the best outcome, and why?

_____

_____

3.  Tim just had to put his dog down. It is really tough for Tim because he thought of his dog as his best friend for the fifteen years that he was alive. Tim has been sober for eight years now, but all he wants now to help him deal with the pain is a drink. Over the last eight years, he has taken great pride in his sobriety because, when he was drinking, he tended to act out aggressively or violently against others. His friends are all gone for the weekend, either on trips or visiting family members out of town. Tim calls his dad to talk about the dog. His dad cut the phone call short because he had an important business partner on the other line. Tim feels alone. He drives to the nearest bar and sits in his car for a while.

Based on the scenario, identify the problem that would require a decision:

_____

_____

Identify three solutions to Tim's problem:

Solution A: _____

Solution B: _____

Solution C: _____

Of the solutions you have identified, which gives Tim the best outcome, and why?

_____

_____

_____

# Section 7:
# Stress Management

# STRESS MANAGEMENT

All forms of distress are ever-present in society and in our personal lives. How we react to and cope with these stressors can have a positive or negative impact on our mental, emotional, physical, and spiritual well-being. With all the pursuits, interests, and ventures that we take on, it is not logical to expect anyone to eliminate all stressors from our lives. In this section, we will help you identify your personal stressors, the negative impact that they have on your life, and techniques that you can implement that will help you cope more effectively.

# Objectives

At the end of this section, the participant will be able to
1.  identify stressors in your personal life,
2.  identify stress reduction techniques, and
3.  practice, in a classroom setting, stress reduction.

# Stress Management

Being "stressed out" is a universal human phenomenon. More often than not, individuals use the word *stress* to indicate negative experiences that make us feel overwhelmed. Yet, considering stress to be exclusively negative in nature gives us a false impression of its true nature. Stress can be defined as the "set of emotional, physical, and cognitive reactions to a change." When we consider it in its full form, stress is more about our ability to cope with change than it is about whether that change makes us feel good or bad. Change occurs frequently in our ever-demanding environment, and stress is largely the most common response we have to it. Thinking about stress in this way shows that it is not necessarily always bad, and sometimes it can be good.

There are two types of stress: eustress and distress. Below are the physiological effects on the human body of eustress and distress:

| EUSTRESS | DISTRESS |
|---|---|
| Elevated heart rate | Elevated heart rate |
| Release of endorphins | Release of endorphins |
| Perspiration | Perspiration |
| Muscle tension | Muscle tension |
| Elevated blood pressure | Elevated blood pressure |
| Increased insulin (sugar) | Increased insulin (sugar) |
| Increased cholesterol | Increased cholesterol |
| Heightened senses | Heightened senses |

So what's the difference between eustress and distress? Although the body reacts the same to both types of stress, eustress and distress are entirely different in their effects on our mental state. Think of eustress as a term for positive stress and distress as a term for negative stress. The difference between the two lies in our perception of the stressor. According to Dr. Harry Mills, Dr. Natalie Reiss, and Dr. Mark Dombeck, eustress, or positive stress, "motivates, focuses energy, is short-term, is perceived as within our coping abilities, feels exciting, and improves performance". Distress, or negative stress, "causes anxiety or concern, can be short- or long-term, is perceived as outside of our coping abilities, feels unpleasant, decreases performance, and can lead to mental and physical problems" (Mills).

On the next page, you will find a graph depicting the effects of eustress versus distress.

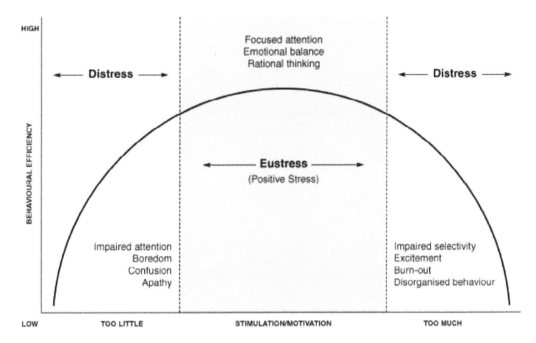

Stressors are the reason for our stress response to particular circumstances. Generally, people tend to categorize these stressors in their minds as negative or positive, which sparks their reaction to the stressor as distress or eustress.

## Identification of Stressors

Negative personal stressors
- Death of a spouse or other family member
- Separation or divorce
- Life threatening health issues (oneself or loved ones)
- Injury or illness (oneself or loved ones)
- Being abused or neglected
- Conflict in interpersonal relationships
- Financial problems
- Unemployment
- Sleep issues
- Children's problems at school
- Legal troubles
- Work-related problems

Positive personal stressors
- Receiving a promotion or raise at work
- Starting a new occupation
- Marriage
- Buying or selling a home
- Having a child
- Relocating to an unfamiliar area
- Going on a vacation
- Demands of holiday seasons
- Retirement
- Taking educational classes
- Learning a new hobby

---

Stressors do not have to be restricted to situations where problems arise from an external source. Internal attitudes or behaviors also cause distress.

Frequent internal sources of distress include:
Fears or phobias
Extensive worry over future events
Repeated thought patterns
Idealistic and unfeasible expectations

Habitual behavior patterns that may cause stress include:
Overscheduling
Failure to be assertive
Procrastination
Failure to plan ahead

---

The right attitude can convert a negative stressor into a positive one.—Hans Selye.

---

 Laughter is usually the best natural medicine to respond to stress. It lowers levels of cortisol, adrenaline, and epinephrine, which are stress-aggravating hormones; and it releases feel-good hormones, such as dopamine.

# Why Are Some People Better at Handling Stressful Situations Than Others?

If given the same stressful situation, one person might break down at the face of it, while another might attack the problem head on without a shudder. What makes some people so good at dealing with stress? The answer lies in how they **perceive** the stress and the stressor. The concept of "self-efficacy" is important in understanding how stressors are perceived by some as debilitating and others as tolerable. Self-efficacy is the belief one has in his or her own effectiveness in competently dealing with life's tasks and hardships, particularly stressful situations that arise. Some individuals truly believe in their own abilities to endure and manage themselves. Research has shown that having high levels of self-efficacy decreases people's risk of experiencing feelings of distress by increasing their sense of control over the stressors they encounter.

The understanding of being in control acts as an important shield against negative stress. When people feel they are not in control, they start to feel stressed, even if they are in control and simply don't know it.

By perceiving negative stressors as being within the realm of our control, we can effectively transform a distress situation into a eustress situation, freeing us from the burden of anxiety and all the harmful consequences that accompany it.

So how do we reduce distress? We can never get rid of all of it, so let's look at simple ways to minimize its impact on our lives.

**FUN FACT**  According to research, the major cause of stress in nearly all countries surveyed is money. The least stressed countries are Russia, France, and Italy.

# Healthy Ways to Reduce Distress in Our Lives

Every day we are faced with potential distressful situations. We don't have to let these situations overwhelm our mental, emotional, physical, and spiritual well-being. Here are some tips that will help you relax and enjoy a more fulfilling life.

**Clarify your values.** Discover what is truly important to you. Ask yourself, "If I only had six months left to live, what would I need to accomplish before dying?" Conduct an honest analysis of your character strengths and weaknesses. Develop a checklist and get to work.

**Learn to relax.** Start by finding a quiet space and blot out all distractions (radio, TV, and other noise producers). Try it for at least 15–20 minutes per day and build up your endurance to one hour of quiet time every day. Listen to soothing music. Meditate. Pray. Reflect on where you want to be in life, and determine how you are going to get there. Stop wasting time worrying about past mistakes and what might happen tomorrow.

**Be aware of your negative self-talk.** We can't deny that we all engage in some form of self-talk every day and that much of it is self-criticism that focuses heavily on past mistakes. Seek balance in your self-talk. Emphasize your positive character traits.

**Exercise regularly.** Check with your primary care physician. Find some form of physical exercise that you can participate in three times a week, for about twenty minutes each time. Walking, stretching exercises, sit-ups, chin-ups, jumping jacks, skipping rope, etc. are all simple forms of exercise that cost little or nothing to participate in. Quit making excuses!

**Eat nutritional, balanced meals.** Discover the foods that serve to fuel your body and help you function at your best. Identify foods that sap your energy, and either use them in moderation or remove them from your diet altogether. If you aren't sure what these foods are, consult a certified nutritionist or perhaps a health food store employee.

**Create balance in all seven areas of your life:** social, mental, spiritual, physical, career, family, and financial. Using a vehicle as a metaphor—if a tire is under- or overinflated, a battery is not fully charged, the brakes are worn, you use the incorrect oil, or the fuel is tainted, then the vehicle will not and cannot perform efficiently.

Stop using harmful chemicals. The need to acquire temporary emotional and mental relief through artificial means accounts for the popularity of nicotine, alcohol, caffeine, sugar, and drugs. Find alternative, healthier ways to improve your emotional and mental well-being.

# Physical Techniques for Reducing Stress

It is common to become overwhelmed by all the obligations and commitments looming over our heads at any moment. When we feel overcome by these distresses, we must not let them defeat us. To effectively combat stress in the moment, we need to activate the body's natural relaxation response. Here are some of the most effective relaxation techniques. Relax, you deserve it. And it takes less time than you think!

1. Observing your breath carefully
2. Counting your breaths
3. Head rolling in both directions
4. Slow shoulder shrugs
5. Tightening and releasing muscle tension slowly
6. Scalp and neck massage
7. Self-massage
8. Meditation
9. Using a heat wrap around neck and shoulders
10. Laughing
11. Listening to relaxing music
12. Yoga
13. Biofeedback
14. Physical exercise
15. Tai chi
16. Repetitive prayer
17. Keep a gratitude journal
18. Neurofeedback Therapy

# Stress Reduction Contract

Improving our overall quality of life can come in large part from reducing the stress in our lives. It is something that we must commit ourselves to in full. By signing this statement, you agree to work toward a more stress-free personal environment. You are the only one that can sustain it and the only one that can violate its conditions.

I will control/reduce the impact of at least three stressors in my life by doing the following:

## Stressor 1
Actions:

_____

_____

_____

## Stressor 2
Actions:

_____

_____

_____

## Stressor 3
Actions:

_____

_____

_____

Signature _____

Chewing gum eases, not only the jaw, but stress as well. Ancient Mayans and Greeks chomped on resin gum; stress sure has been around a long time!

# Section 8:
# Coercive Control

# COERCIVE CONTROL

Annually, more than ten million men and women in the United States report experiencing physical or sexual assault by their partners. Twenty people per minute are physically abused by a partner. At the same time, approximately three million men in the United States report experiencing physical assault by their partners, with few men reporting being the victims of sexual assault. It is estimated that for every reported incident, just as many or more go unreported. The pervasiveness of domestic violence in our society is a direct result of coercive control within relationships. Coercive control is the emotional and psychological abuse of a partner, through threats and restrictions, as well as physical violence.

We, as humans, have a tendency to either coerce others or allow ourselves to be coerced by others, which inevitably leads to mistreatment and an imbalance of power in relationships. In this section, we will learn about the lasting impact that coercive control has on the individual and his or her partner. We will develop a strategy to provide ourselves with lasting and healthy relationships going forward.

# Objectives

At the end of this section, the participant will be able to
1.  verbalize a clear understanding of coercive control and its impact on society,
2.  identify past situations when you have used coercion,
3.  identify past situations when you have been the target of coercion, and
4.  develop a self-improvement action plan.

# Understanding Coercive Control

A social epidemic facing American society involves the aggressive use of coercion to control the attitudes and the behaviors of others. Coercive acts may include manipulation, humiliation, isolation from friends and family members, controlling finances, degradation (verbal and physical), punishment, stalking, physical abuse (hitting, slapping, pushing, shoving), sexual abuse, emotional and mental abuse, monitoring someone's mail, and other situations where one individual uses power to control someone else. We know that this is an important social issue when criminal and behavioral research has repeatedly documented the continued increase in frequency and severity of coercive behaviors. Researchers have discovered that no one is immune from coercive controls. It can be found among all age groups, socioeconomic levels, ethnic and cultural groups, career fields, etc.

It is human nature—a frailty, if you will—that we are compelled to either coerce others to agree with our point of view or to succumb to coercion by others. Reflect back on your life and consider how someone with real or perceived power over you has tried to control what you think and do. These may include your parents, siblings, teachers, youth group leaders, community leaders, law enforcement officers, spiritual leaders, employers, supervisors, etc. Now, recall the people that you have used coercive control over. It's not a one-way street. When used properly, power establishes boundaries and enforces moral, legal, and ethical codes. When used for personal gain, it causes unnecessary pain to others.

Some perpetrators of coercive control are conditioned to believe that their actions are not harmful. Some individuals tend to stop their behaviors when they learn how harmful they have been to other people. Conversely, there are individuals who are fully aware of the harm they cause, yet continue their behaviors. Some coercers are so proficient at controlling the attitudes of others that the targets of their abuse believe that they caused or deserved the abuse. This section will help you understand the perspective from both the coercer and coerced person's point of view, and identify what actions you can take to stop the cycle of violence.

Coercive control isn't a one-time event. It evolves over an extended period of time and involves the coercer repeatedly mistreating the partner through intimidation and even violence. By instilling and reinforcing fear, the perpetrator controls a partner's thoughts and behaviors. While the reader may jump to the conclusion that perpetrators are traditionally male and victims traditionally female, there is an increasing number of cases where the male is the victim and female the perpetrator. Coercive control can also be found among same-sex couples.

We can always find some small amount of manipulation even in healthy interpersonal relationship. Coercive relationships, however, are very harmful. These relationships lack shared goals (personal and career), decision-making, mutual respect, and financial equality. One partner's needs are considered to be of greater importance. There is an absence of equanimity. This section seeks to instill in you an understanding of the importance of establishing equality in order to maintain and enjoy a healthy relationship

# The Life of a Coerced Partner

Research has found a number of commonalities among persons who are susceptible to being coerced. Feelings of powerlessness, hopelessness, and helplessness, together with a low self-concept, are present among coerced partners. Many were emotionally, mentally, physically or sexually abused as children. When in an abusive relationship, they continually suffer mental, emotional, and sometimes physical pain and sexual abuse. They live in constant fear of upsetting their partner. Individuals who seek help to escape from an unhealthy relationship report that their abuser was, at the beginning, overly attentive and kind. Once the person has been won over, subtle changes occur. It may involve criticizing the partner's family members, friends, coworkers, or others with whom the partner has a close relationship. The coerced partner is eventually isolated from others, allowing the coercer to assume a position of power. The coerced person is no longer free to speak her or his mind and is not permitted to question her or his partner's decisions. Mental and emotional trauma is accompanied by physiological complaints—difficulty sleeping or oversleeping, poor appetite or overeating, headaches, nausea, and digestive tract issues. When a child in the home is also the target of abuse, the parent who is feeling powerless to intercede—for fear that the abuse will escalate—can be charged with failure to protect the child. In worst-case scenarios, the coerced partner can seek refuge at a domestic violence shelter, or join the ranks of the homeless. Individuals who have escaped a toxic environment often describe their daily existence as "walking on egg shells."

# The Life of a Coercive Partner

Just as the targets of coercive control can be found throughout all segments of our society, so can coercive partners. One's age, social status, class, ethnicity, career field, cultural origins, or educational level cannot predict who will become an abuser. Research has identified two common factors among individuals who seek to control others. Either they were raised in an environment where coercive control was practiced by the adults around them or they were victims of coercion themselves. Or perhaps it is a combination of both. The two most common theories that explain coercive control are gender inequality and superiority. Both of these theories help to explain, albeit irrationally, why one group has unfettered access to social capital (education, career, resources, etc.) while others are blocked from gaining access. The first theory posits that men are of greater value to society than women. This is reflected in the number of male versus female elected officials, chief operating officers of Fortune 500 companies, pay for professional athletes, and women generally being paid less than men with the same skill set. The theory of superiority is simply that one group believes itself to be superior to all others and therefore is justified in wielding power indiscriminately. In both instances, those with power will do whatever it takes to remain in power and feel very threatened when the powerless overtly question the status quo.

## A Serious Social Problem

Research conducted by the United States Department of Justice discovered that 37% of women who were admitted to emergency rooms for violence-related injuries were found to have been abused by an intimate partner. Annually, more than four million women in the USA report experiencing physical or sexual assault by their partners. It is estimated that for every reported incident, just as many or more go unreported. At the same time, approximately three million men in the USA each year are victims of physical assault, with few men reporting being the victim of sexual assault. Research repeatedly suggests that one in four American females will be the victims of sexual molestation at least one time in their lives.

More than 60% of victims reported that the violence occurred in the home. Abuse is the third leading cause of homelessness among families, according to the Department of Housing and Urban Development. Coercive control is reported to cost more than thirty-seven billion dollars every year, in the form of law enforcement involvement, legal work (attorneys, court costs, etc.), medical and mental health treatment, and lost work productivity.

Coercion is also a burgeoning social concern among US high school and college students. Females between the ages of sixteen and twenty-four experience the highest rate of intimate partner violence—almost triple the national average. Violent behavior typically begins between the ages of 12 and 18, with the severity of intimate partner violence often greater in cases where the pattern of abuse was established in adolescence. Violent relationships in adolescence and young adulthood can have serious ramifications by placing their victims at a high risk for substance abuse, eating disorders, risky sexual behavior, attempted suicide, and further victimization. Around 50% (half) of all youth who attempted suicide reported that they had been the victims of both partner violence and rape, compared to 12.5% of non-abused girls and 5.4% of non-abused boys who reported attempting suicide.

Approximately 1.5 million high school students every year experience some type of abuse from an intimate partner. According to the Oklahoma State Department of Education, one in three youths report being the victim of verbal, emotional, physical, or sexual abuse by a partner. One in ten high school students in the United States report that they were intentionally hit, slapped, or otherwise physically harmed by a girlfriend or boyfriend.

## Why Is Coercive Control Allowed to Continue?

The coercive partner enjoys the power that he or she has over others, and doesn't want to relinquish this power. Victims of abuse who report being abused place themselves at a high risk for retaliation. Here are some of the known impediments to stopping coercive control:

- A victim of abuse is at a very high risk of being murdered the first 24 hours after leaving their abuser. The victim is not always believed, even by some professionals and law enforcement.
- The victim is often blocked from accessing community resources.
- The abuser has no respect for differences of feelings and opinions of others. The abuser cannot or will not apologize when they make mistakes.
- The abuser is seldom willing to listen to another's point of view.
- The abuser does not seek assistance or advice from others, even when needed.

# What Can I Do to Reduce the Effects of Coercive Control?

Each and every one of us must commit to actively work toward reducing the incidences of coercive control, especially when it inflicts serious mental, emotional, and physical pain on the victims. We must commit ourselves to identifying the perpetrators, referring them to the appropriate professional, encouraging them to accept responsibility for their actions, and helping them to stop their destructive behaviors. We must commit to protecting the victims of abuse by identifying and helping them tap into the community support network. Most importantly, we must commit to educating our children about the effects that coercive control has on individuals, to prevent them from being perpetrators or victims.

## Points to Ponder

Since coercion takes on many forms, and none of us are immune from taking advantage of another person, it is time to get really honest with yourself. Review the following situations, and respond honestly to each one. Honesty will provide you with an understanding of how to improve yourself, and to avoid conflict in the future.

- Is stopping a parent from seeing his or her children because that individual failed to pay child support a form of coercive control?

Yes _____     No _____

Have you done this to someone else? Explain in detail.

Has someone done this to you? Explain in detail.

- Is withholding child support because your former partner is in a new relationship a form of coercive control?

Yes _____     No _____

Have you done this to someone else? Explain in detail.

Has someone done this to you? Explain in detail

- Is withholding your true thoughts and feelings from a partner a form of coercive control?

Yes _____ No _____

Have you done this to someone else? Explain in detail.

Has someone done this to you? Explain in detail.

- Is monitoring someone's phone calls, text messages, and mail a form of coercive control?

Yes _____ No _____

Have you done this to someone else? Explain in detail.

Has someone done this to you? Explain in detail.

- Is it a form of coercive control when someone asks you for a favor and you respond that you will do the favor on the condition that he or she does a favor in return?

Yes _____ No _____

Have you done this to someone else? Explain in detail.

Has someone done this to you? Explain in detail.

- Is the practice of withholding sexual favors from your partner after you have had a serious argument a form of coercive control?

Yes _____ No _____

Have you done this to someone else? Explain in detail.

Has someone done this to you? Explain in detail.

- Is the practice of demanding sexual favors from a partner a form of coercive control?

Yes _____ No _____

Have you done this to someone else? Explain in detail.

Has someone done this to you? Explain in detail.

- Is withholding affection from someone that you love, because you are upset with that person, a form of coercive control?

Yes _____          No _____

Have you done this to someone else? Explain in detail.

Has someone done this to you? Explain in detail.

- Is telling children not to obey a stepparent a form of coercive control?

Yes _____          No _____

Have you done this to someone else? Explain in detail.

Has someone done this to you? Explain in detail.

- Is shouting at children when they don't obey you a form of coercive control?

Yes _____          No _____

Have you done this to someone else? Explain in detail.

Has someone done this to you? Explain in detail.

- Is lying to someone, in order to get them to do something they might not do if they knew all the facts a form of coercive control?

Yes _____          No _____

Have you done this to someone else? Explain in detail.

Has someone done this to you? Explain in detail.

- Is telling your partner that she or he must behave in certain ways in order to remain in a relationship with you a form of coercive control?

Yes _____        No _____

       Have you done this to someone else?

       Has someone done this to you?

- Is shouting at a partner when he or she has done something that you do not approve of a form of coercive control?

Yes _____        No _____

       Have you done this to someone else? Explain in detail.

       Has someone done this to you? Explain in detail.

# Self-Assessment

Now that you have identified situations in which you have used coercion on others and situations in which others have used coercion on you, this exercise asks you to find alternative actions to previous coercive behavior in order to create a plan for healthy relationships in the future. Please describe the last three times you have coerced someone into conforming to your attitudes or behaviors. We will then analyze these past circumstances to determine if there was a better way to solve that particular problem.

1. The last time that I coerced someone into conforming to my attitudes or behaviors was when I . . .

_____

_____

_____

_____

_____

When I was in this coercive situation, I felt . . .

_____

In these particular circumstances, the victim of my coercion was . . .

_____

I imagine that, because of my coercion, the victim would have felt . . .

_____

Instead of using coercion in this situation, I could have solved my problem by . . .

_____

_____

_____

"No one has the right to place one human being in a position of power over another." –Wendy McElroy

2.  Another time when I coerced someone into conforming to my attitudes and/or behaviors was when I…

_____

_____

_____

_____

_____

When I was involved this coercive situation, I felt . . .

_____

In these particular circumstances, the victim of my coercion was . . .

_____

I imagine that, because of my coercion, the victim would have felt . . .

_____

Instead of using coercion in this situation, I could have solved my problem by . . .

_____

_____

_____

"Sometimes it is difficult to realize or hear our own prejudices and own up to their existence. Admitting there is a problem is the first step to recovery"—Thomas Hodge

3.  Another time when I coerced someone into conforming to my attitudes and/or behaviors was when I...

_____

_____

_____

_____

_____

When I was involved this coercive situation, I felt . . .

_____

In these particular circumstances, the victim of my coercion was . . .

_____

I imagine that, because of my coercion, the victim would have felt . . .

_____

Instead of using coercion in this situation, I could have solved my problem by . . .

_____

_____

_____

When reviewing the three situations you described above, are there any similarities that you were able to identify such as circumstances, attitudes, or behaviors?

Examples might include the following:

- Alcohol was involved.
- Illegal substances were involved.
- A particular victim was the target of the coercion or anger.
- Each instance occurred before or after a stressful or traumatic event.
- The attitudes were the same (resentment, bitterness, hostility).
- The behaviors were the same (punching, breaking things, pushing, etc.).

In order to reduce or eliminate these kinds of coercive behaviors, we must identify the similarities in the instances when they occur. Then we can work on improving our behaviors through the elimination of these similarities. What similarities can you find in the three situations you described above?

Similarities between Situations 1, 2, and 3:

1. _____

2. _____

3. _____

4. _____

5. _____

Finally, please describe what actions you are going to take to avoid coercive behaviors and circumstances in the future: _____

_____

_____

_____

Avoiding coercive acts protects us and others from needless suffering.
Relationships free of coercive attitudes and behaviors provide each partner
with a sense of strength, balance, security, and unification of purpose.

# The Coercers' Commitment to Change

By initialing each item, and signing my name at the bottom, I hereby commit to making the following positive changes in my life.

_____I accept full responsibility for my past coercive behaviors.

_____I accept that I have hurt other people by my coercive actions.

_____I will make amends to all the people I have hurt, wherever possible.

_____I will stop coercing other people for my personal gain.

_____I will be considerate of the feelings of other people.

_____I will be considerate of the opinions of other people.

_____I will be less critical of other people's attitudes.

_____I will be less critical of other people's behaviors.

_____I will help protect other people from being the target of coercion.

_____I will teach other people how to protect themselves from coercion.

Date _____     Signature _____

# The Coerced Targets' Commitment to Change

By initialing each item and signing my name at the bottom, I hereby commit to making the following positive changes in my life.

_____I accept that I allowed myself to be the coerced into doing things against my will.

_____I accept that I allowed someone else to control my thoughts.

_____I accept that I allowed someone else to control my feelings.

_____I accept that I allowed someone else to take control of parts of my life.

_____I will let go of all resentments I have toward people who coerced me in the past.

_____I will stop letting people talk me into doing things that I don't want to do.

_____I will follow my intuition when I think someone is trying to manipulate me.

_____I will use the language of feelings when communicating with others.

_____I will help protect other people from being the target of coercion.

_____I will teach other people how to protect themselves from coercion.

Date _____        Signature _____

# Section 9:
# Conflict Resolution

# CONFLICT RESOLUTION

Conflict resolution occurs when individuals address a real or perceived wrong and come to an understanding in a peaceful manner. The conflict may be personal, financial, political, or emotional. When a dispute arises, often the best course of action is negotiation, not anger, aggression, or violence. The latter reactions only cause more harm to both parties involved in the conflict. In this section, we will identify conflicts in our past that could have been resolved in different ways, and we will practice resolving conflicts in an effective manner in order to improve our resolution abilities in the future.

# Objectives

At the end of this section, the participant will be able to
1. identify past situations when you experienced conflict with others,
2. identify the factors that preceded the conflicts,
3. identify the negative consequences that evolved from the conflicts, and
4. practice, in a classroom setting, effective conflict resolution.

# CONFLICT RESOLUTION

Conflict is defined by Dr. Ron Fisher as "an incompatibility of goals or values between two or more parties in a relationship, combined with attempts to control each other and antagonistic feelings toward one other" (Fisher 1977). Conflict arises between people in every variety of human relationship and in each kind of social setting. Standing alone, conflict is neither good nor bad. However, the way in which conflict is handled will decide if it is constructive or destructive.

Conflict has the potential to be destructive, to both individuals and to society, or it can motivate us to make positive social changes. Consider the civil rights movement of the 1960s, a time fraught with fighting, riots, burnings, and the destruction of personal and public property. American society was faced with two courses of action—continue the status quo, which would only serve to escalate tensions, or form a coalition to resolve people's differences. Fortunately, cooler heads opted for the latter, with passage of the Civil Rights Act of 1964. While the Civil Rights Act (as amended) did not eradicate social unrest, it did serve to open up dialogue between the opposing factions.

As a nation, we constantly struggle to understand the beliefs held by various ethnic, cultural, religious, and social groups, especially when they differ from our own. The purpose of this section is not to resolve our society's social ills but to help you to learn and implement effective conflict resolution skills. The two primary sources of conflict that we will be addressing here are power and values.

Power enters into all instances of conflict since the object is to try and control one another. Each side of the conflict wants to maintain the amount of influence that it exerts in the relationship. One party wants to remain strong, requiring the other party to remain weak. When both parties are unwilling or unable to give ground an impasse occurs, which only serves to fuel existing tensions (a lose-lose situation). There are occasions when one party plays the power card; that is, when one side has real or perceived control over the other and makes a unilateral decision. This action generally results in one person claiming victory and the other person admitting defeat (a win-lose situation). The ideal outcome is when two parties respect one another's position and arrive at a mutually agreeable decision (a win-win situation).

The clashing of values occurs when there exists incompatibility in personal ideologies or preferences. Each side is convinced that their beliefs are right, which means that the opposing side must, therefore, be wrong. The parties' belief systems are so ingrained that they are incapable of viewing the situation from another's point of view.

Whether the source of conflict is power or values, neither party wants to seek a compromise, thinking that varying from their position is a sign of weakness which the other party can use against them at a later date.

As conflict escalates, those around them are often forced to take one side or the other. This creates a polarizing effect, with each party becoming even more adamant that their position is the superior one. When this occurs, it often requires the intervention of a mediator to help them arrive at a solution that is amenable to both parties.

In addition to addressing the sources of conflict, we must also present an overview of the different levels of conflict. For the purpose of this section we will be discussing three types: interpersonal, role, and intergroup.

Interpersonal conflict is when two people have incompatible needs, goals, or beliefs, or when they view an issue from very different perspectives. If two parties to a relationship have a strong need for power, there is no way that either will have their needs met. Common tactics used to gain the upper hand in interpersonal power struggles include deception and evasion, threats, emotional blackmail, rewards and punishment. When these ploys don't work, people revert to flattery and ingratiation. A subset of interpersonal conflict is personality conflict, which involves much stronger differences in motives, personal values, or styles in dealing with people—differences that cannot be resolved, even with the assistance of a mediator.

Role conflict involves confusion regarding the defining of one another's roles, expectations, and individual responsibilities. Confusion, disenchantment, emotional intensity, and friction are often the byproducts of such ambiguity. In personal relationships, couples who fail to share expectations of their various roles in a relationship, especially if they begin to cohabitate, operate under false assumptions. The root of friction in relationships is centered on unmet needs, most commonly identified as the absence of mutual respect, open and honest communication, financial security, mutual support of one another's personal and professional goals, and intimacy.

Organizational effectiveness consultants and social psychologists have long known that the most successful organizations are those with a new hire orientation program. The program ensures that all employees understand their role, the roles of coworkers, and how they fit together to achieve the organization's mission. These individuals report that they are comfortable in their new environment, and supervisors report that they are productive within thirty days of hiring. Conversely, individuals who are not properly oriented to their new environment report feeling lost, insecure, and full of self-doubt. It may be 120 to 180 days before they feel that they are an integral part of the organization—that is, if they remain. Untold billions of dollars are lost in lack of productivity, and an organization's reputation is sullied as the result of high employee turnover.

Intergroup conflict involves groups of people who possess very different belief systems, which can most commonly be found between ethnic, racial, or religious groups, management and workers, departments or divisions within the same company, etc. Individuals identify with a specific group and develop stereotypes (oversimplified, often false, negative beliefs) about members of the opposing group. Stereotypical assumptions lead to blaming others for their own problems—scapegoating—enlarging an existing gulf between two disparate groups of individuals. Intergroup conflict leads to overt and covert acts of a discriminatory nature that block certain groups or members of those groups from accessing social capital (economic and social parity, political power, educational achievement, etc.).

 The shortest war on record took place in 1896 when Zanzibar surrendered to Britain after 38 minutes.

# Roots of Tension and Anxiety

For most people, the following events or conditions are experienced as stressful. Distress leads to unnecessary conflicts with others. We must work to understand and be aware of the roots of our tensions and anxieties in order to avoid lashing out at others as a result of them. If we fail to do so, we risk encouraging negative attitudes and behaviors to exist in our lives.

1.   Becoming overwhelmed, overworked, overburdened, or overscheduled
2.   Being ill or having a loved one become ill
3.   Death of a loved one
4.   Divorce or divorce of a loved one
5.   Problems in relating to a husband, wife, partner, parent, child, boss, coworker, or friend
6.   Having a baby
7.   Financial hardship or indebtedness
8.   Business reversal
9.   Being overextended financially or being unemployed
10.  Having too many commitments at once
11.  Having burnout—too little rest, sleep, or recreation
12.  Surgeries, injuries, or accidents
13.  Dental work
14.  Overly strenuous exercise, overexertion, or overtraining without being in shape for it
15.  Exercising without stretching or preparing the body
16.  Overeating or eating the wrong foods
17.  Having chronic pain or illness
18.  Being overweight or being underweight
19.  Smoking, alcohol, drug abuse, or caffeine/stimulant addiction
20.  Environmental stress such as smog, traffic, or noise pollution

---

| Negative Attitudes | Negative Behaviors |
|---|---|
| Having to be perfect | Trying to change others |
| Having to be the best | Carrying grudges |
| Having to be right | Playing the role of victim |

# Methods of Conflict Resolution

It is evident that ongoing conflict between two parties, groups and multiple groups results in a lose-lose situation. What we will address here is how to achieve a win-win resolution, where most of every party's needs are met. This can be best achieved through the application of assertive communication techniques.

Before going any further, let's conduct a brief review of what you learned in the "Effective Communication" section of this workbook. You learned that an assertive communicator does not attack another person's ideas or beliefs. You also learned that effective communicators modulate their tone of voice, use language that the other person understands, establish and maintain effective eye contact, remain open-minded and receptive to new ideas, use negotiation and compromise to achieve a mutually-agreed upon solution, and express themselves in an open, honest, and nonthreatening manner.

Let's also conduct a brief review of the "Coercive Control" section. In the following scenarios, ask yourself, "Do I feel that I am being manipulated to commit to something I don't need or want?" "What exactly is making me feel this way?" "What actions can I take to resolve the impasse?"

Now, ready or not, it is time for you to put your knowledge to a test! Take a deep breath. Relax your body. Think happy thoughts. Smile. We know that you can do this!

**Scenario 1.** Your partner tells you that it is time to buy a new vehicle.

Your partner presents the following points: The car has over 100,000 miles on the odometer, things are about to break down, it has quite a few dings, the color has faded, it looks beat up, the upholstery is shot, your children don't like the vehicle, he or she is embarrassed being seen driving that junk heap, and he or she can afford a new vehicle if you cut back on other expenditures (e.g., dining out, gym membership, cable and Internet, going on a vacation, cut back on snacks, etc.).

You present the following points: If taken care of, the vehicle will last another 30,000 to 50,000 miles; you had your friend check it out, and all the main equipment is operational; the vehicle is paid for; it has all new tires; a friend of yours can hammer out the dings; it won't cost much to have it repainted; the rear seat has two to three small tears, which can be easily repaired; you really don't care what other people think; you need the gym memberships and cable and Internet access; and the vehicle is functional—it meets your transportation needs.

Scenario 2. Your partner earned an associate's degree before you met and now would like to pursue a bachelor's degree at a local college. To finish the degree in three years, your partner will have to be a three-quarter-time student, requiring a minimum of two courses per semester, including the summer months. You have two children, ages two and four. At present, your partner has been a stay-at-home parent. There are no relatives nearby who could watch your children, so you would have the additional expense of childcare. You would be expected to assume a greater parenting role and increased responsibility for household chores.

Your partner presents the following points: staying at home all day with the children is good for them, but he or she needs to engage with other adults; the children need to socialize with other children their age; you are eligible for free prekindergarten care run by the city; the children are well-adjusted; he or she may be eligible for scholarships; he or she may be eligible for a monthly stipend; when your partner is done, he or she starts earning $30,000 to $35,000 a year, plus benefits.

You present the following points: your partner is the one who wanted to be a stay-at-home parent—you think that he or she is going back on his or her word; you need to know that the city's prekindergarten program is accredited by a legitimate agency; you need to know what hours they will be there; you agree that your children are well-adjusted and that they need to be around children their own age; you need to know if all the courses will all be daytime, nighttime, a mixture of day and night, or if the partner will have to take weekend classes; you are not sure you can juggle work, taking a more active parenting role and taking care of the children.

Scenario 3. Your partner is tired of living in a small town (7,000 population) and wants to relocate to a large city. You have two children entering middle school. You have lived in the same house since the children were born. You both are involved in your church, and volunteer in your small community.

Your partner presents the following points: there is more to do in the city (museums, a zoo, theaters, an aquarium, parks, fine dining, etc.); he or she is tired of everyone knowing our business; the city schools are much better; the children want to move—there's nothing for them to do here; the city offers a variety of athletic programs, for boys and girls; the church people are a bunch of busybodies; there are more couples our own age in the city; you will have more opportunities for volunteer work in the city.

You present the following points: country life is better for your health; you can always drive to the city if you want to visit the museums, theaters, etc.; the children won't know anybody—it will be a hard adjustment for them; okay, you grant that the children will have more opportunities to play sports; the people in our little church may be busybodies, but they are very kind; city folks just aren't as friendly as country folks; you would have to sell our house before you can even consider moving, and the market is slow right now; you really like volunteering at the Grange Hall; the cost of living in a city is much higher than the country; home and car insurance rates will go up; you don't like the city crime rate.

# Conflict Resolution Case Studies

Now it is time to test how much you have learned about resolving conflicts. Below are five scenarios in which you are tasked with conflict resolution. Work diligently as if the scenarios given were real situations in your life. Make sure to give the steps you would take, in detail, to settle the disputes and an explanation as to why you took this particular path to solve the issue. Good luck!

Case 1: You have been contracted, at the rate of $100 per hour to resolve a dispute between two parties. You will only be paid when both parties agree that you have permanently found a solution for the conflict.

The scene: A homeowner has signed a written agreement with a contractor to have a covered, screened-in 10'×20' lanai, with concrete pad, added to his home. Since the contractor met his responsibilities, the homeowner paid him in full. Thirty days later, a sudden thunderstorm occurred. The lanai roof leaked in several places. The homeowner called the contractor to complain. They have been unable to agree on who should be responsible for correcting the problem. You know that the homeowner and contractor are not related in any way. You also do not have any bias toward or against either party. As a third-party mediator, it is your duty to come up with an action plan that both parties will agree upon in order to fix the lanai roof and keep both parties satisfied. What corrective action plan will you create?

Plan:

_____

_____

_____

_____

_____

Why did you choose this particular corrective action plan?

_____

_____

_____

_____

_____

Case 2: You are the supervisor at a large company. Part of your job is ensuring that all employees are working well together. Any disputes between employees come to you. If you do not handle the situation properly, human resources files a report with your supervisor, explaining that the issue has not been resolved and that assistance is needed.

The scene: Bob is the office prankster. Most of his jokes are in good taste, but occasionally, he can be inappropriate. Since Mary, who is African American, started in the department, Bob has made a daily habit of sharing a joke about blacks to everyone in the department, usually in an open setting. After hearing one of his offensive jokes, you take him into the office to counsel him. After you mention that his jokes are offensive, Bob stated that he had his "first amendment right to freedom of speech" and that you are attempting to violate his rights. Bob is a good employee; it would be damaging to the company to fire him. But his jokes are no longer acceptable in the office. What corrective action plan will you create?

Plan:

_____

_____

_____

_____

_____

FUN FACT

Since 1495, no 25-year period has been without war.

Why did you choose this particular corrective action plan?

_____

_____

_____

_____

_____

Case 3: You are a lawyer hired for a case involving a couple that had recently filed for divorce. It is your job to sort out the paperwork and resolve any final debates between the two. You are not paid your fee unless both parties have signed the divorce papers, thus both accepting all terms to the separation.

The scene: You have been trying to sort out all the financial issues between the couple for a few weeks now. Eric and Alyssa cannot come to terms about who should have possession over their set of fine China dishware. The dishware is originally Alyssa's grandmother's fine China. Her grandmother gave the set to Alyssa and Eric as a gift on their wedding day. Alyssa thinks she should have the entire set for herself, while Eric thinks that they should split the set between the two of them. They have asked you about the matter because they are looking to you to take a side. You must give your advice on the issue in order to finish the divorce papers and receive your payment. What corrective action plan will you create?

Plan:

_____

_____

_____

_____

_____

 The very first bomb that the Allies dropped on Berlin in World War II killed the only elephant in the Berlin Zoo.

Why did you choose this particular corrective action plan?

_____

_____

_____

_____

_____

# Section 10:
# A New Beginning

# A NEW BEGINNING

In this workbook, you have reflected and built upon the ways to guide you toward a happier and healthier lifestyle. Now you must consider how this learning can help you in the future. With these new skills, you have the opportunity to start anew. Continuing the negative attitudes or behaviors you possessed prior to this program will harm your relationships, health, and career. You must commit to making positive changes in your lives if you are to achieve balance in your emotional, mental, physical, and relational well-being.

# Objectives

At the end of this section, the participant will be able to

1. verbalize a clear understanding of how continuing your negative behaviors affect your interpersonal relationships, your health, and your career,
2. identify those positive life changes you have made during this course,
3. identify those positive life changes that you will make in the future,
4. develop clear and measurable objectives to achieve improved physical health,
5. develop clear and measurable objectives to achieve improved mental health, and
6. develop clear and measurable objective to achieve improved emotional health.

# I CHOOSE NOT TO BE A VICTIM

A critical part of moving on after processing past mistakes and committing to positive change is the acceptance of responsibility for one's own future well-being. By signing this statement, you are contracting with yourself to gain control over your life. The burden for upholding this contract rests solely on you. You are the only one that can sustain it and the only one who can violate its conditions. It is time to move forward!

✔ I acknowledge that I have made some healthy and some unhealthy choices in my life.

✔ I accept that I cannot blame others for the choices that I have made.

✔ I accept that I am responsible for what I choose to think and feel.

✔ I accept that I can choose the direction in my life.

✔ I accept that I am responsible for my emotional well-being.

✔ I accept that I can only help others if I am healthy.

✔ I accept that I am responsible for my own physical well-being.

✔ I accept that I am responsible for improving myself—emotionally, mentally, physically, and spiritually.

✔ I accept that I am responsible for my spiritual well-being.

✔ I resolve to seek help if I find myself unable to resolve my own issues, past or present.

✔ I resolve to process and finally let go any of my past abuse that I suffered at the hands of others.

✔ I accept that I have to let go of the past in order to be happy.

Signature: _____

# A NEW BEGINNING

This section is a review of everything that you have learned in this course. We congratulate you on the many positive lifestyle changes you have made thus far and hope that this visual representation helps you realize everything that you've accomplished. However, your work is not done. Within this section, you will also identify what tasks remain unfinished and any new tasks you discover during your section reviews.

Section 1: Building Character. I have made the following positive changes:

1. _____

2. _____

3. _____

I commit to making the following changes in the future:

1. _____

2. _____

3. _____

Section 2: Gender and Society. I have accomplished the following:

1. _____

2. _____

3. _____

I commit to making the following changes in the future:

1. _____

2. _____

3. _____

 In 2010, there were an estimated 45.9 million adults (aged 18 or older) in the United States with a mental illness. Mental illnesses are more common than cancer, diabetes, or heart disease.

*Section 3*: Building a Healthy Lifestyle. I have accomplished the following:

1. _____

2. _____

3. _____

I commit to making the following changes in the future:

1. _____

2. _____

3. _____

*Section 4*: Effective Communication Skills. I have accomplished the following:

1. _____

2. _____

3. _____

I commit to making the following changes in the future:

1. _____

2. _____

3. _____

*Section 5*: The Language of Feelings. I have accomplished the following:

1. _____

2. _____

3. _____

I commit to making the following changes in the future:

1. _____

2. _____

*Section 6:* Making Rational Decisions. I have accomplished the following:

    1. _____

    2. _____

    3. _____

I commit to making the following changes in the future:

    1. _____

    2. _____

    3. _____

*Section 7:* Stress Management. I have accomplished the following:

    1. _____

    2. _____

    3. _____

I commit to making the following changes in the future:

    1. _____

    2. _____

    3. _____

*Section 8:* Coercive Control. I have accomplished the following:

    1. _____

    2. _____

    3. _____

I commit to making the following changes in the future:

    1. _____

    2. _____

Section 9: Conflict Resolution. I have accomplished the following:

1. _____

2. _____

3. _____

I commit to making the following changes:

1. _____

2. _____

3. _____

 "But there's a begin ning in an end, you k now? It's true that you can't reclaim what you had, but you can lock it up behind you. Start fresh."
—Alexandra Bracken, The Darkest Minds

# Congratulations

*T*hank you for investing so much of your time and energy taking the many steps along the Pathways Toward Non-Aggression that we have set out for you. We hope that it was a productive and life-changing experience. The journey is far from over. There are many more steps to take. It is your responsibility to determine what these are, and to keep moving in a forward direction. We leave you with one thought . . . .

*"The truth is that our finest moments are most likely to occur when we are feeling deeply uncomfortable, unhappy, or unfulfilled. For it is only in such moments, propelled by our discomfort, that we are likely to step out of our ruts and start searching for different ways or truer answers."* — M. Scott Peck, M.D.

# REFERENCES

Ajmera, Ripa. (2015, September 4). The Effects of Poor Communication. Livestrong. Retrieved from: http://www.livestrong.com/article/80901-effects-poor-communication/.

Alcohol Facts and Statistics. (2017). National Institute on Alcohol Abuse and Alcoholism

(NIAAA). Retrieved from: https://www.niaaa.nih.gov/alcohol-health/overview-alcohol-consumption/alcohol-facts-and-statistics.

Alcohol's Effects on the Body. National Institute on Alcohol Abuse and Alcoholism (NIAAA). Retrieved from: https://www.niaaa.nih.gov/alcohol-health/alcohols-effects-body.

Alcohol, Tobacco and Other Drugs. (2016). Substance Abuse and Mental Health Services Administration (SAMHSA). Retrieved from: http://www.samhsa.gov/atod.

Alcohol & Your Health. (2016). National Institute on Alcohol Abuse and Alcoholism (NIAAA). Retrieved from: https://www.niaaa.nih.gov/alcohol-health.

Alexandra Bracken Quotes. (2014). Good Reads. Retrieved from: http://www.goodreads.com/quotes/1152795-but-there-s-a-beginning-in-an-end-you-know-it-s.

American Psychiatric Association. (2013). Diagnostic and Statistical Manual of Mental Disorders (5th ed.). Washington, DC: American Psychiatric Association.

Beebe, S., Beebe, S., Redmond, M., Geernick, T., & Salem-Wiseman, L. (2015). Interpersonal Communication – Relating to Others (6th ed.). Toronto: Pearson.

Bern, S. (1981). Gender schema theory: A cognitive account of sex typing. Psychological Review, Vol. 88(4), 354-364.

Blackstone, Amy. (2003). Gender Roles and Society. Human Ecology: An Encyclopedia of Children, Families, Communities, and Environments. Santa Barbara: Miller, Lerner, and Schiamberg.

Boboltz, Sara. (2014, April 16). 9 Facts That Prove Traditional Definitions Of Gender Roles Are Bullsh*t. Huffington Post. Retrieved from: http://www.huffingtonpost.com/2014/04/16/gender-facts-traditional-roles_n_5115265.html.

Botham, Noel. (2010, November 1). The Mega Book of Useless Information. London, UK: John Blake Publishing Ltd.

Breedlove, Mark S. (2011, March 11). Biological Psychology: An Introduction to Behavioral, Cognitive, and Clinical Neuroscience. Content Technologies, Inc. Brewer, H. (undated). List of Gender Stereotypes. Health Guidance. Retrieved from: http://www.healthguidance.org/entry/15910/1/list-of-Gender-Stereotypes.html.

Bussey, K. & Bandura, A. (1999). Social cognitive theory of gender development and Differentiation. Psychological Review, Vol. 106(4), 676-713.

Cabansag, Clifford. (2017). Alcohol Use Disorders. American Board of Addiction Medicine (ABAM). Retrieved from: https://namiswoh.org/wp-content/uploads/sites/31/2014/11/Alcohol-Use-Disorders-PowerPoint.pdf.

Carter, Sherrie. (2012, October 20). Emotions Are Contagious—Choose Your Company Wisely. Psychology Today. Retrieved from: http://www.psychologytoday.com/blog/high-octane-women/201210/emotions-are-contagious-choose-your-company-wisely.

CDC: Adult Obesity Facts. (2016). Centers for Disease Control and Prevention. Retrieved from: http://www.cdc.gov/obesity/data/adult.html.

Commonly Abused Drugs Charts. (2016). National Institute on Drug Abuse. Retrieved from:

https://www.drugabuse.gov/drugs-abuse/commonly-abused-drugs-charts.

Cox, Tony. Brain Maturity Extends Well Beyond Teen Years. (2011, October 10). National Public Radio. Retrieved from: http://www.npr.org/templates/story/story.php?storyId=141164708.

DASH diet: Healthy eating to lower your blood pressure. (2016). The Mayo Clinic. Retrieved from: http://www.mayoclinic.org/healthy-lifestyle/nutrition-and-healthy-eating/in-depth/dash-diet/art-20048456.

Dating Abuse Statistics. (2016). Love Is Respect. Retrieved from: http://www.loveisrespect.org/resources/dating-violence-statistics/.

Definition of Character; Definition of Value. (2017). Oxford Dictionaries. Retrieved from: http://en.oxforddictionaries.com/definition/character.

Dietary Guidelines. (2016). Center for Nutrition Policy & Promotion (CNPP). Retrieved from: https://www.cnpp.usda.gov/dietary-guidelines.

Domestic Violence Statistics. (undated). Iris Domestic Violence Center. Retrieved from: http://www.stopdv.org/index.php/statistics/.

Drugs of Abuse. (2016). National Institute on Drug Abuse (NIDA). Retrieved from: https://www.drugabuse.gov/drugs-abuse.

Eat Clean and Get Lean. (2015). Emmaus, PA: Prevention Magazine, September 2015.

Eat Clean, Stay Lean. (2016). Emmaus, PA: Prevention Magazine, April 2016.

Eckes, T. & Trautner, H. (2000). The Developmental Social Psychology of Gender. New York: Psychology Press.

Effective Communication. (2016). Help Guide. Retrieved from: https://www.helpguide.org/articles/relationships/effective-communication.htm.

Effective Decision Making. (2016). Skills You Need. Retrieved from: http://www.skillsyouneed.com/ips/decision-making.html.

Ehrensaft, M.K. & Vivian, D. (1999). Is Partner Aggression Related to Appraisals of Coercive Control by a Partner? Journal of Family Violence, 1999, 14:251.

Eleven Facts About Mental Health. (undated). Do Something. Retrieved from: http://www.dosomething.org/us/facts/11-facts-about-mental-health.

Ellin, Abby. (2016, July 11). With Coercive Control, the Abuse is Psychological. The New York Times. Retrieved from: https://well.blogs.nytimes.com/2016/07/11/with-coercive-control-the-abuse-is-psychological/?_r=0.

Energy Drinks. (2016). National Center for Complementary and Integrative Health. Retrieved from: https://nccih.nih.gov/health/energy-drinks.

Exercise 101: The 7 Benefits of Regular Physical Activity. Tuskegee University. Retrieved from: http://www.tuskegee.edu/sites/www/Uploads/files/Staff%20Senate/The%207%20Benefits%20of%20Exercise.pdf.

Facing Fears: Eustress vs. Distress. (2014). Climbing in the Kitchen. Retrieved from:
https://climbinginthekitchen.com/2014/09/09/can-you-tell-the-difference-between-eustress-and-distress-and-how-your-interpretation-may-be-holding-you-back-from-success/.

Fact Sheets – Alcohol Use and Your Health. (2016). Centers for Disease Control and Prevention. Retrieved from: https://www.cdc.gov/alcohol/fact-sheets/alcohol-use.htm.

Fact Sheets – Binge Drinking. (2015). Centers for Disease Control and Prevention. Retrieved from: https://www.cdc.gov/alcohol/fact-sheets/binge-drinking.htm.

Fact Sheets - Caffeine and Alcohol. (2015). Centers for Disease Control and Prevention. Retrieved from: https://www.cdc.gov/alcohol/fact-sheets/caffeine-and-alcohol.htm.

Fielden, John S. (1964, May). "What Do You Mean I Can't Write?". Harvard Business Review. Retrieved from: https://hbr.org/1964/05/what-do-you-mean-i-cant-write.

Fisher, B. & Alberti, R. (2014). Rebuilding – When Your Relationship Ends (3rd ed). Atascadero, CA: Impact Publishers, Inc.

Fisher, Ron. (1977). Sources of Conflict and Methods of Conflict Resolution. Semantic Scholar. Retrieved from:
http://pdfs.semanticscholar.org/c79d/9b7849528d3fa2170d33b6382f7da2b77a11.pdf.

Food Labeling Guide. (2016). U.S. Food & Drug Administration. Retrieved from:
http://www.fda.gov/Food/GuidanceRegulation/GuidanceDocumentRegulatoryInformation.

Hans Selye Quotes. (2017). Brainy Quote. Retrieved from:
https://www.brainyquote.com/quotes/quotes/h/hansselye381383.html.

Harris, J. (1995). Where is the child's environment? A group socialization theory of Development. Psychological Review, Vol 102(3), 458-489.

Healthy Eating Plate. (2016). T. H. Chan School of Public Health, Harvard University Medical

School. Retrieved from:
http://www.hsph.harvard.edu/nutritionsource/healthy-eating-plate/.

Health Information. (2016). U.S. National Library of Medicine. Retrieved from:
https://www.nlm.nih.gov/hinfo.html.

Healthy Living. (2016). American Heart Association (AHA). Retrieved from:
http://www.heart.org/HEARTORG/HealthyLiving/Healthy-Living/.

Heneman, K., & Zidenberg-Cherr, S. (2007). Nutrition and Health Info Sheet: Energy Drinks.
Retrieved from: http://anrcatalog.ucanr.edu/pdf/8265.pdf.

Henna Inam Quotes. (2017). Good Reads. Retrieved from:
http://www.goodreads.com/author/quotes/13919759.Henna_Inam.

Hogan, Meghan. (2014). The Dangers of Impulsive Decision Making. Good Choices Good
Life. Retrieved from: http://www.goodchoicesgoodlife.org/choices-for-real-life-real-living/
the-dangers-of-impulsive-decision-making/.

How to Understand and Use the Nutrition Facts Label. (2017). U.S. Food and Drug
Administration. Retrieved from: https://www.fda.gov/food/ingredientspackaginglabeling/
labelingnutrition/ucm274593.htm.

Infographic: Listening facts you never knew. (2013, June 12). Ragan. Retrieved from:
http://www.ragan.com/Main/Articles/Infographic_Listening_facts_you_never_
knew_46838.

John C. Maxwell Quotes. (undated). GoodReads. Retrieved from:
https://www.goodreads.com/author/quotes/68.John_C_Maxwell.

Leaper, C. & Friedman, C. K. (2007). The Socialization of Gender. Chapter 22, Handbook of
Socialization: Theory and Research, edited by J. Grusec & P. Hastings.

Lehnardt, Karin. (2017, March 20). 41 Interesting Facts about Human Emotion. Fact Retriever.
Retrieved from: http://www.factretriever.com/human-emotion-facts.

Maglaty, Jeanne. (2011, April 7). When Did Girls Start Wearing Pink? Smithsonian Magazine.
Retrieved from: http://www.smithsonianmag.com/arts-culture/
when-did-girls-start-wearing-pink-1370097/.

Mehrabian, Albert. (1972, July). *Silent Messages: Implicit Communication of Emotions and
Attitudes*. Boston, MA: Wadsworth Publishing Company.

Mental and Substance Use Disorders. (2016). Substance Abuse and Mental Health Services
Administration (SAMHSA). Retrieved from: http://www.samhsa.gov/disorders.

Merriam-Webster Dictionary. (2016). Merriam-Webster Dictionary. Retrieved from: http://www.merriam-webster.com/.

Mills, H., Reiss, N., Dombeck, M. (2008). Types of Stressors (Eustress vs. Distress). MentalHelp.net. Retrieved from: https://www.mentalhelp.net/articles/types-of-stressors-eustress-vs-distress/.

Mills, H., Reiss, N., Dombeck, M. (2008, June 30). Self-Efficacy and the Perception of Control in Stress Reduction. MentalHelp.net. Retrieved from: https://www.mentalhelp.net/articles/self-efficacy-and-the-perception-of-control-in-stress-reduction/.

National Coalition Against Domestic Violence (NCADV). (2016). Retrieved from: http://www.ncadv.org/learn-more/statistics.

National Intimate Partner and Sexual Violence Survey. (2010). National Center for Injury Prevention and Control: Centers for Disease Control and Prevention. Retrieved from: https://www.cdc.gov/violenceprevention/pdf/nisvs_executive_summary-a.pdf.

National Survey on Drug Use and Health (NCADV). (2016). Retrieved from: http://www.ncadv.org/learn-more/statistics.

Nicholson, Christie. (2012, June 9). Testosterone Promotes Aggression Automatically. The Scientific American. Retrieved from: https://www.scientificamerican.com/podcast/episode/testosterone-promotes-aggression-aut-12-06-09/.

Nutrition and Health. (2016). The Mayo Clinic. Retrieved from: http://www.mayoclinic.org/healthy-lifestyle/nutrition-and-healthy-eating/basics/healthy-diets/hlv-20049477

Nutrition Source. (2016). Harvard School of Public Health, Harvard Medical School. Retrieved from: https://www.hsph.harvard.edu/nutritionsource.

Obesity, Definition. (2017). The Mayo Clinic, Diseases and Conditions. Retrieved from: http://www.mayoclinic.org/diseases-conditions/obesity/basics/definition/con-20014834.

Paul, Marla. (2014, April 2). Morning Rays Keep Off The Pounds. Northwestern University. Retrieved from: https://news.northwestern.edu/stories/2014/04/morning-rays-keep-off-the-pounds.

Sodium: How to Tame Your Salt Habit. (2016). The Mayo Clinic. Retrieved from: http://www.mayoclinic.org/healthy-lifestyle/nutrition-and-healthy-eating/in-depth/sodium/art-20045479.

Sodium in Diet. (2017, May 17). The New York Times Health Guide. Retrieved from: http://www.nytimes.com/health/guides/nutrition/sodium-in-diet.

Solomon, Jamie. (2004). Gender Identity and Expression in the Early Childhood Classroom: Influences on Development Within Sociocultural Contexts. Retrieved from: http://www.naeyc.org/publications/vop/gender-identity-and-expression.

Stark, E. (2007). Coercive Control: The Entrapment of Women in Personal Life. Oxford University Press.

Stark, E. (2012). Looking Beyond Domestic Violence: Policing Coercive Control. Journal of Police Crisis Negotiations, vol. 12(2), 199-217.

Stress Management. (2016). Being Assertive: Reduce stress, communicate better. Retrieved from: http://www.mayoclinic.org/healthy-lifestyle/stress-management/in-depth/assertive/art-20044644.

The Benefits of Walking. (2015). Emmaus, PA: Prevention Magazine, January 2015.

The Food Guide Pyramid. (1992). Center for Nutrition Policy and Promotion. Retrieved from: http://www.cnpp.usda.gov/sites/default/files/archived_projects/FGPPamphlet.pdf.

The Incredible Dr. Pol (2016). National Geographic Wild. Retrieved from: http://www.google.com/webhp?sourceaids=chrome-instant&rlz=1C1CHWA_enUS605US605&ion=1&espv=2&ie=UTF=8#q=national%20geographic%20wild

The truth about fats: the good, the bad, and the in-between. (2015). Harvard Health Publications. Retrieved from: http://www.health.harvard.edu/staying-healthy/the-truth-about-fats-bad-and-good.

Thomas Hodge Quotes. (2016). Good Reads. Retrieved from: http://www.goodreads.com/quotes/7609327-sometimes-it-is-difficult-to-realize-or-hear-our-own.

Trauma and Violence. (2016). Substance Abuse and Mental Health Services Administration (SAMHSA). Retrieved from: http://www.samhsa.gov/trauma-violence.

Twenty Interesting Facts About Stress. (undated). Examined Existence. Retrieved from: http://examinedexistence.com/20-interesting-facts-about-stress-2/.

Underage Drinking. (2016). Substance Abuse and Mental Health Services Administration (SAMHSA). Retrieved from: http://www.samhsa.gov/underage-drinking-topic.

Vagianos, Alanna. (2015, February 13). 30 Shocking Domestic Violence Statistics That Remind Us It's An Epidemic. The Huffington Post. Retrieved from: http://www.huffingtonpost.com/2014/10/23/domestic-violence-statistics_n_5959776.html.

Vincent Van Gogh Quotes. (2016). Good Reads. Retrieved from: http://www.goodreads.com/quotes/75899-great-things-are-not-done-by-impulse-but-by-a.

War Fast Facts. (2010). Did you know? Retrieved from: http://didyouknow.org/fastfacts/war/.

What Can I Eat? (2016). American Diabetes Association (ADA). Retrieved from: http://www.diabetes.org/food-and-fitness/food/what-can-i-eat/.

Wendy McElroy Quotes. (2015). Good Reads. Retrieved from: http://www.goodreads.com/quotes/7039858-no-one-has-the-right-to-place-one-human-being.

Your Healthiest Year Ever. (2015). Emmaus, PA: Prevention Magazine, January 2015.

Zeratsky, K. (2016). Can energy drinks really boost a person's energy? The Mayo Clinic. Retrieved from: http://www.mayoclinic.org/healthy-lifestyle/nutrition-and-healthy-eating/expert-answers/energy-drinks/faq-20058349.

Thom Glaza, Ed. D., M.A.

Melanie Mason

Thomas "Thom" G. Glaza, EdD, has worked as an addictions specialist and mental health counselor for over thirty-five years. He has a doctorate in counseling psychology and a master's degree in sociology. He served twenty-four years in the US Navy, retiring as a chief petty officer and a Vietnam veteran. Chief Glaza was the first counselor assigned to a naval vessel. He developed and facilitated a variety of workshops in the navy—leadership and management, cross-cultural relations, substance abuse, conflict resolution, race relations—and trained personnel at the command level to conduct ongoing training. Chief Glaza is a Vietnam veteran. Dr. Glaza is founder and CEO of Tri-County Counseling and Life Skills Center Inc., in North Port, Florida. He is a Florida-licensed mental health counselor, certified clinical trauma professional, nationally certified custody evaluator, certified master's level addictions professional, and certified sex offender treatment specialist.

Melanie Mason is an incoming student to the University of Florida's Clinical Mental Health Counseling Master's/Ed.S. program. She graduated from the University of Florida in April of 2017, with a major in criminology and minors in both history and Spanish. She has studied in Spain to gain fluency in Spanish. She attended the University of Cambridge, in England, to research and author a research paper on the emergence of the London Metropolitan Police Force. Ms. Mason is a crime analyst intern at the Gainesville Police Department in Gainesville, Florida. She volunteers her time at numerous charitable organizations, including the Child Advocacy Center, Big Brothers Big Sisters, and Teen Court of Manatee County. Ms. Mason has conducted research on fear of crime in elderly citizens, as well as the prominence of mental health issues within the criminal justice system, for the University of Florida and has worked as an intern for the Tri-County Counseling and Life Skills Center in North Port, Florida, since May 2016. She plans on gaining her dual licensure in mental health counseling and marriage & family counseling, then moving into a Ph.D. in Criminology upon completion of her graduate program.

CPSIA information can be obtained
at www.ICGtesting.com
Printed in the USA
BVHW09s0113080818
523879BV00005B/9/P